# Junior Johnson Brave in Life

# Junior Johnson

### BRAVE IN LIFE

# Johnson

TOM HIGGINS AND STEVE WAID

INTRODUCTION BY CALE YARBOROUGH
DESIGN BY TOM MORGAN

DAVID BULL PUBLISHING

## Acknowledgments

I lovingly dedicate this book to my family. To my children, Robert, my namesake, who brought me the greatest moment of my life when he was born; and my beautiful daughter Meredith, who is most certainly an angel. And to my loving wife, Lisa, who is my best friend.

A special recognition to my sister Annie Mae, who has always had a smile no matter what adversity. To all the guys who have worked for me over the years—we certainly had some good times. And I'd especially like to thank all the race fans, both young and old.

—Junior Johnson

The authors and the publisher would like to thank Clay Call, David Chobat, Terry Hall, Mike Hill, Don Hunter, Nigel Kinrade, Buz McKim and the NASCAR archives, Dozier Mobley, Hank Schoolfield, Mike Staley, Jeff Stutts, and T. Taylor Warren for making their photographs and archives available. Thanks also to Bob Zeller for generously sharing his research materials.

Library of Congress Cataloging-in-Publication Data
Higgins, Tom, 1937-
    Junior Johnson : brave in life / by Tom Higgins and Steve Waid : foreword by Cale Yarborough.
      p. cm.
   ISBN 1-893618-00-5 (softcover)
    1. Johnson, Junior, 1931- . 2. Automobile racing drivers--United States Biography.   I. Waid, Steve, 1948- . II. Title.
III. Title: Brave in life.
GV1032.J55H54    1999
796.72'092—dc21
[B]
ISBN 1-893618-00-5

Printed in Hong Kong

Book design: Tom Morgan, Blue Design, Portland, ME (www.bluedes.com)

10 9 8 7 6 5 4 3 2

David Bull Publishing
4250 E. Camelback Road
Suite K150
Phoenix, AZ 85018

602-852-9500
602-852-9503 (fax)

www.bullpublishing.com

**Page 2:** Junior and his car show the wear and tear of dirt-track racing in 1959. Junior won five of his twenty-seven starts that year, finishing eleventh in the points standings. (Daytona Racing Archives)

**Opposite:** Junior (No. 3) won the pole and Fred Lorenzen (No. 28 at left) was in the number two spot to start the fourth annual World 600 at Charlotte Motor Speedway in 1963. Junior led 77 laps before a beer bottle cut his right rear tire on the 397th of 400 laps, allowing Lorenzen to coast to victory. (Don Hunter)

**Pages 6-7:** A.J. Foyt drove three times for Junior in 1966. Foyt's best finish was eleventh at the season-opening Motor Trend 500 at Riverside, and his last race for Junior was at the Daytona 500 one month later. (Pal Parker)

**Page 8:** In 1956, Junior's Pontiac roared around Daytona's north turn at a speed too fast even for Junior to handle. He reached upwards of 110 mph during the race, and lost control on lap 30, rolling over twice before coming to a stop. Junior escaped the wreck unhurt through the back window, his race helmet in hand. He received $25 for placing fortieth in the race. (Southern MotoRacing)

# CONTENTS

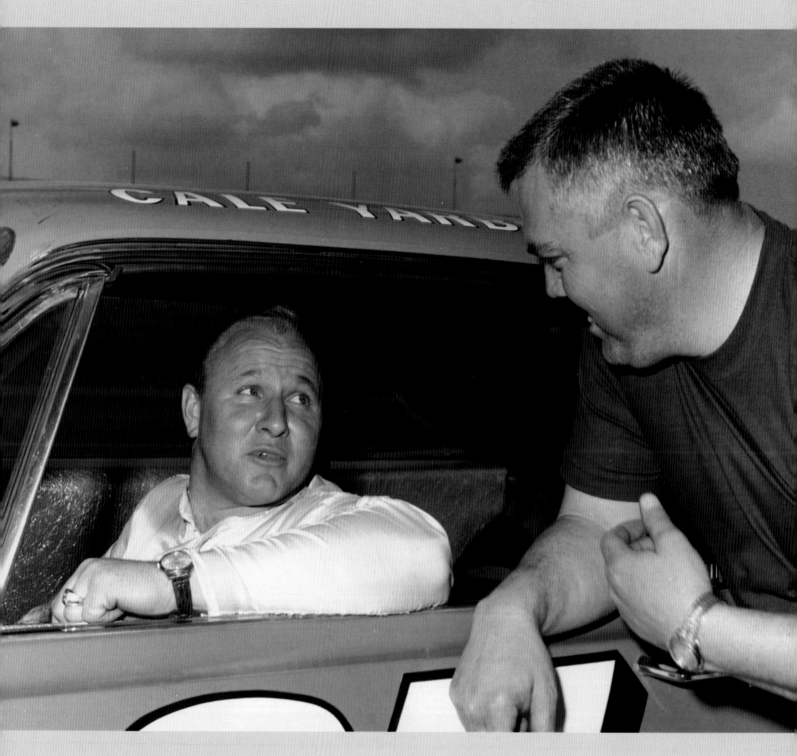

In 1965, Junior and Cale Yarborough
talk before an unidentified race. Before
they won three consecutive Winston Cup
Championships as team owner and
driver, Junior and Yarborough competed
against each other on the track from
1962 to 1966. (Daytona Racing Archives)

**Junior's stories about his days as a whiskey hauler are riveting and often hilarious. Running moonshine groomed Junior for a racing career because he learned about cars and speed.**

# FOREWORD BY
## CALE YARBOROUGH

## I can honestly say the years I spent with Junior Johnson were fun.

We had far more than a driver-team owner relationship. I never really thought I worked for Junior. We were more like partners. We worked closely together when it was time to race and we shared a lot of time together away from the race track. We had a great relationship.

My years with Junior started in 1973 and ended after the 1980 season, and they were the best of my career. I'm proud of all I was able to accomplish with Junior and I'm especially proud of the three consecutive NASCAR Winston Cup championships we won from 1976 through 1978. I have no idea what roads my career would have followed if I hadn't been able to drive Junior's cars, so I consider myself especially fortunate to have spent those years with him.

I think Junior and I were compatible because we shared similar backgrounds. Neither one of us started out with a lot, but we weren't afraid to work hard to make something of ourselves. We both took chances. We both made sacrifices. In the end, both of us succeeded because we made the most of the talents we had.

I know Junior's story well, and it is a fascinating one. His stories about his days as a whiskey hauler are riveting and

often hilarious. Running moonshine groomed Junior for a racing career because he learned about cars and speed—and he learned those lessons well. When it came to racing, Junior was a no-nonsense competitor. He was bold and aggressive. His style was one I tried to emulate and Junior liked that about me. That's another reason we worked so well together.

Junior never failed at anything he tried. He was considered the best whiskey hauler. He ranks as one of NASCAR's greatest drivers, and he is one of the most successful team owners of all time. Junior's a man who rose from humble beginnings to become one of the most recognizable figures in all of American automobile racing. That's truly remarkable.

I am glad that Junior Johnson's story is now being told. It goes beyond a simple success story. It's a tale of late-night, high-speed chases with the law, rough-and-tumble racing on dirt and asphalt, and the often tense business of team ownership.

As I said, it's a fascinating story.

And I am proud to be a small part of it.

—Cale Yarborough

# CHAPTER ONE

Junior Johnson was concerned about mule power, not horsepower, that Saturday morning in early summer of 1949.

The corn planted a few weeks earlier by Junior, his brothers, and their father on the family's farm at Ingles Hollow near the hamlet of Ronda had grown to a height of about a foot, and the crop needed to be plowed.

Junior was handling the chore, working the long rows back and forth behind a favorite old mule, guiding the animal through its task with gentle tugs on a pair of long reins and soft, drawled commands of "Gee" and "Haw."

Junior was at the far reaches of the field, where the rolling cropland turned to the steep terrain of the Brushy Mountains, when he noticed L.P., his older brother. Junior plowed his way back to a point nearer the road.

"I was very surprised to see him," Junior recollects. "A race was scheduled that day at North Wilkesboro Speedway, the new track nearby that Enoch Staley and some other local fellers were trying to get going. L.P. had been looking forward to that race and had left home early for the track. I asked L.P. why he had come back to the farm. I remember him being all excited. He said that Enoch and his partners were trying to organize a preliminary race to entertain the big crowd that had gathered. They were

## "I was brave in life. I took more chances."

Left: Races were often held at North Wilkesboro, a popular dirt track near Junior's hometown. Note that no guardrail or wall protected those on pit road from the action on the track along the backstretch. (Southern MotoRacing)

Above right: Junior (far left in car No. 1) leads a Sportsman race at North Wilkesboro in a 1939 Ford Standard. In second place, in the two-tone car on the inside, is Hardin Minton, a part-time employee of the track who, like Junior, hailed from Wilkes County. (Mike Staley collection)

**Left:** Visibility was a problem for drivers and spectators alike on the North Wilkesboro dirt track. Fans—here found hanging from the trees—often had to bathe or shower several times to cleanse the dust from their bodies. (Southern MotoRacing)

**Opposite:** Junior receives a trophy for winning a Sportsman Division event at North Wilkesboro in 1949. At right is his friend and fellow driver, Gwyn Staley, who lost his life in a crash at Richmond Raceway in 1958 during a NASCAR convertible race. (Mike Staley collection)

going to match the boys from around the area in their whiskey-haulin' cars.

" 'Junior,' L.P. said, 'I want you to drive my car.' Well, gettin' the chance to do that tickled me to death. I told L.P. that he would have to wait 'til I put the mule up and then went to the house to get my shoes."

Junior, then 17, had been plowing the cornfield barefoot.

"When me and L.P. got to the track, we saw that word about the preliminary race had spread fast," Junior says. "The best I recall, Enoch and his people had gathered fifteen to twenty cars. Everybody who was going to be involved in the race, as far as I know, was mixed up in bootlegging. I knew I had a chance to do real well. L.P. had a dandy car, a 1940 Standard Ford. It was a liquor car. He hauled in it every night.

"They got the race goin', and I really enjoyed it. The speedway was a dirt track at that time, so it was sort of like driving on the back roads in the mountains of western North Carolina, which were mostly unpaved in those days."

Junior remembers the track tearing up as the race progressed, "becoming rougher than a plowed field." He finished second to Gwyn Staley, a brother of Enoch. Gwyn won two races at NASCAR's top level before being killed in a crash at Richmond, Virginia, in 1958.

"I might could have won except a lapped car sort of crowded me late in the race. Remember, we were inexperienced about racin' in circles, and the boy driving that car didn't see me. Anyway, I really enjoyed the competition. The spectators enjoyed it, too, so a circuit was started for our little ol' cars. There were a few rules, like requiring roll bars, but overall it was pretty rustic."

A lot of guys who would later make names for themselves in racing got started in this division that sprang out of that spur-of-the-moment preliminary show at North Wilkesboro.

Among the best known of this bunch were drivers who became champions like Ned Jarrett and Ralph Earnhardt.

Thus began Junior Johnson's racing career, which was to make him a legend in his own time.

Robert Glenn Johnson Jr. was born in Ingles Hollow, North Carolina, on June 28, 1931. Ingles Hollow is a crossroads in Wilkes County, not far from the town of Ronda.

The Johnson family home was located in the countryside, east of North Wilkesboro, just a short distance away from Highway 421, the main artery between the city and its much larger neighbor, Winston-Salem.

Junior was the fourth of seven children born to Robert Glenn and Lora Belle Johnson. Lewis Preston was the oldest, followed by Ruth, Fred, and then Junior. Annie Mae and Shirley followed. The youngest son, Dwight, died at age nine of appendicitis.

A year later, Junior himself got appendicitis, but he, unlike his younger brother, was able to get the proper emergency medical treatment.

Named after his father, the younger Johnson naturally was called "Junior." He wasn't referred to as "Robert Jr." but simply "Junior."

The Johnsons were a typical family living at the foothills of the North Carolina mountains in the grasp of the Great Depression. They made their living primarily off the land, raising crops and livestock. Robert Glenn also ran a sawmill. As Junior recalls, the family didn't have much, but compared with the hardscrabble lives some Wilkes County families led, the Johnsons prospered. However, they, too, felt the sting of the Depression.

"I remember 'long about 1934 or '35, when I was just a toddler, we had what we called the 'Watkins Man,' " Junior recalls. "This was a traveling salesman who came around and peddled stuff like rosebud salve, liniments,

Left: Junior (right), age eight, stands with his older brother Fred (left), age 10, and younger brother Dwight (middle), age six, in front of the Johnson family home in 1939. Dwight was stricken with appendicitis a few years after this photograph was taken, and died at age nine. (Junior Johnson collection)

Below: Robert Glenn and Lora Belle Johnson worked a variety of jobs to contribute to the household income. But increasingly, in the face of the Great Depression, moonshining became the family's biggest moneymaker. (Junior Johnson collection)

sage, and stuff like that. At a certain time of year, he would come around and he'd have the seeds you needed to plant for your crops, stuff like beans, lettuce, all that stuff.

"My daddy always bought the seeds he would need for his garden. This one time when he bought some seeds, the cost was thirty-five cents.

"The Watkins Man came back in about two weeks with the seed. Well, when he came up to the house, my daddy and two neighbors were talking. Among the three of 'em, they couldn't raise thirty-five cents to pay for that seed.

"Even as I got older, that episode stuck in my mind," Junior says. "It always reminds me of how much of a struggle life was back then."

The Johnsons might have followed the path to poverty had not Robert Glenn Johnson plied a trade that was against the law.

He was a moonshiner.

Moonshine, also called "corn squeezin's," "white lightning," and "corn likker," is illegally distilled, homemade corn whiskey.

Creating moonshine involves a process of heating a mixture of corn mash and water in a still—a large vat—then gathering and condensing the steam through a twisting maze of pipe. The distilled, clear alcohol is poured into mason jars and packed into cases for transport.

Some moonshiners put cherries or sliced peaches into the clear whiskey, which adds color and a fruity flavor to make Cherry Bounce and peach brandy.

Moonshine is illegal because it is untaxed, unlike the fine Kentucky bourbon made by legitimate certified distillers. Through its Alcohol, Tobacco, and Firearms division, the federal government put as many moonshiners as possible out of business and into prison.

Despite the federal government's position, a moonshiner wasn't considered a criminal by his peers. During the Depression, moonshining was perhaps the best way for a man to generate an income for his family. He was considered about as far removed from an Al Capone–like gangster as one could get.

"You did it for no other reason than money," Junior says. "You knew it was wrong as far as the law was concerned, but what other way, during those times, was there to make money?"

The Wilkes County countryside was littered with stills.

Although the number of moonshiners in Wilkes County couldn't easily be counted, Robert Glenn Johnson's operation was the area's biggest. By Junior's estimate, he built and ran as many as 1,000 stills in his lifetime.

"My daddy ran a big operation. He had several stills going at one time. They built most of 'em back deep in the

Unidentified men lean on a still in Wilkes County in the 1950s. The oven on the left is the "cooker", which boils the corn mash [fermented corn]. The steam and vapor from the corn mash rises through the copper pipe at the top of the cooker into a coil in the first barrel, which is full of cold, running water (notice the opening at the bottom). The cold water causes condensation of the alcohol vapor, which is then collected in the next barrel. This condensation is moonshine. (Clay Call collection)

This Wilkes County still is similar to the stills the Johnson family used to make illegal moonshine in the 1950s. Although he was around it his entire life, Junior says he never drank moonshine except for a few sips. "I just didn't like the taste of it." (Clay Call collection)

# "We thought this was fun," Junior says. "The lawmen didn't. They'd say, 'You damn kids get off them cases.' And we'd say, 'You get outta here. This is our house.'"

Lawmen, known as revenuers, were responsible for catching moonshiners and destroying stills. From left to right are Milt Higgins, Ott Whitson, and Hubert Hollifield shown after busting a still in Yancey County, just west of Junior's home. Higgins holds a coil used to condense the alcohol vapor and direct it into containers. (Tom Higgins collection)

woods, but some of 'em were in basements, and they even built a few of 'em underground. Daddy had many of 'em, but he had to, because when one was found, well, the agents would just blow it up. Daddy couldn't go out of business just because he had a still get blowed up."

Moonshiners had a huge market. The demand for whiskey in the South was tremendous. In most locations, legal whiskey simply wasn't available.

Whiskey could be purchased legally only in state-owned liquor stores, maintained by the Alcoholic Beverage Control Board in the larger cities. A person couldn't get a drink at a restaurant or bar, even in such metropolitan North Carolina cities as Raleigh and Charlotte. Country clubs, private clubs, and a practice called "brown bagging," in which one brought one's own booze to a restaurant and paid for ice and mixers, were the only exceptions.

It was much the same in Georgia, Virginia, South Carolina, and other Southern states. A network of moonshiners who operated in the hills and mountains of the rural South developed to meet the demand.

From a very young age, Junior was familiar with moonshining, even if he couldn't understand fully what it was. Junior remembers: "Daddy had so much whiskey in cases that it was stored throughout the house. It was stacked up in our bedrooms in cases so high we had to climb over 'em to get into the bed."

Occasionally, ATF agents raided the Johnsons' house to confiscate and destroy the stock. To remove the cases stored in the bedrooms, the agents would set up long planks on the stairs, slide the cases down them, then carry them into the yard, where they were smashed into a pile of broken glass. When Junior was about three or four years old, he and some neighbor children used to go to the top of the stairs, hop on top of the cases, and slide right down the planks with them, as though riding a sled.

"We thought this was fun," Junior says. "The lawmen didn't. They'd say, 'You damn kids get off them cases.' And we'd say, 'You get outta here. This is our house.'"

Removing cases from the Johnsons' home became so routine the arrival of the agents was expected. Junior's mother was always prepared and often served them pie and coffee as they destroyed months of work and thousands of dollars of moonshine.

Moonshiners got their name because they only did their work at night, under the light of the moon. This included the trickiest part: delivering the goods to customers. Delivering moonshine required a car that could go very fast and a driver with the nerve and skill to hurtle it along twisting roads in the pitch-black dead of night.

Moonshiners could count on being hunted by ATF agents, called revenuers—or "revenooers," if you adopt Southern pronunciation—driving fast cars with the goal of confiscating moonshine, impounding cars, and putting the moonshiners behind bars. The revenuers also had the task of finding and disabling stills. Any man caught hauling or working a still received swift punishment.

But that didn't deter most moonshiners, and it certainly didn't deter Robert Glenn Johnson. As many times as the law busted up his business, the elder Johnson pressed on. In 1935, federal agents raided the Johnson house and discovered a whopping 7,254 cases of moonshine. It was the single largest inland seizure of illegal whiskey ever made in America, the news wire services reported.

Even that didn't stop Robert Glenn Johnson, or his family.

The influence Junior's father exerted on his son was great. Compared with other children growing up in Wilkes County, Junior had a good life. That was largely because his father worked like a mule all the time, making moonshine, working at the sawmill, or farming.

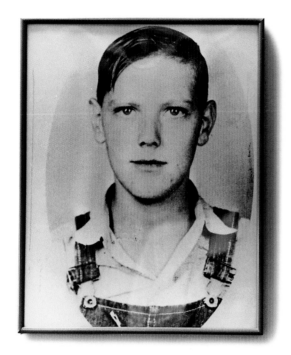

By the time this picture had been taken, Junior, age 15, was already well versed in the business of moonshining. Junior remembers his first moonshine experience, when he delivered empty containers to his father, who was firing the still in the middle of the night. As he walked through the woods in the dark, Junior remembers, "I heard all kinds of boogers. I was a-scared. I wasn't a-scared of the law, I didn't know much about that. I was just a-scared of what was going to jump out and get me." (Junior Johnson collection)

"He reminded me a lot of Robin Hood," Junior says. "It sounds like I'm a-braggin' on him, but I'm really not. Anyone who crossed his path never forgot him. He would give you the last nickel he had if you asked him for it."

From his father, Junior learned early on that whatever he had to do, he had to do it right then. Do it now and don't wait. He wasn't turned loose to find out things for himself; he was always given direction.

"My father would spend time with me, showing me how to do stuff," Junior remembers.

So Junior became adept at performing chores around the house and farm, contributing to the household before he was ten years old. He also became interested in mechanics. When he was around eight years old, Junior decided to learn just what made the Briggs & Stratton engine work on his father's mower. So he took it apart.

"Thing was, I couldn't get it put back together again," Junior says. "I tried hard, but I couldn't do it. I had engine parts stacked up everywhere, and I didn't know where they went." Robert Glenn might have admired his son's curiosity, but he couldn't abide the fact a mower engine was left in ruins.

"I got my hind end wore out," Junior says.

At about the same time he was dismantling mower engines, Junior discovered his love for baseball. He got involved in organized youth leagues in Wilkes County and played regularly, year after year. He developed into a quality left-handed pitcher.

He advanced from Little League to American Legion baseball. To keep his throwing edge, he would often pitch baseballs from the time he came home from school until dark. He began to chase his dream of becoming a major league pitcher, and many thought he had the skills.

But when he was fourteen years old, he broke his left arm in an accident when he overturned a tractor while, as Junior puts it, "acting the fool."

For a long time, he could not throw a baseball. Unable to practice every day and follow the routine he had established, Junior lost interest in his dream of the major leagues.

Social functions in Wilkes County were few. "You made up your own activities," Junior says. "You chose up sides and played games, stuff like that." There were high school sports and the movies. Kids enjoyed the Westerns with Ken Maynard, Roy Rogers, and Gene Autry.

When he was thirteen years old, Junior became friendly with a girl who lived near him. Her name was Flossie, and they soon began to socialize with mutual friends. They married in Las Vegas in 1975, many years after they had established a home in Wilkes County and Junior's racing career had evolved from driving to owning a team.

Junior's schooling was brief. He went to Clingman Elementary School and then attended Ronda High School. After completing the eighth grade (which was part of high school in those days), he dropped out. By his own admission, it was a "damn fool" thing to do.

"I don't really know why I did it," Junior admits. "I was so eager to do my own thing, and that was to make and haul moonshine. That's my excuse. It's a poor one, but back then you didn't need school like you do today."

Robert Glenn himself got through the third grade before he quit school. But Junior considers him one of the smartest men he has ever known. His father was a self-educated man who could read, write, and do math.

Though he withdrew from formal education, Junior admired the intelligence of some of his classmates. "They did very well in life," Junior says. "But I did a lot better. I took more chances. I was brave in life. It's paid off for me as far as finances are concerned."

# 7,100 GALLONS LIQUOR AND 5 STILLS SEIZED

## Huge Haul Is Made By Federal Investigators In Raid In Wilkes County.

## MAY SET NEW RECORD

Seizure of about 7,100 gallons of whisky, 9,150 pounds of sugar, four copper condensers, five complete distilling plants having a combined capacity for the manufacture of 2,000 gallons of liquor each week or virtually twice that amount in case of forcing the capacity, a steam boiler of the upright type, an automobile, more than $1,000 worth of fruit jars, together with such other paraphernalia as cases, cans, filters and funnels, constituted some of the results of week-end raiding activities in Wilkes county of members of the federal alcoholic tax unit, it was learned yesterday following the return of the investigators to Greensboro.

Available information indicates that this was the largest inland seizure of strictly blockade liquor in the entire country, so far as the knowledge of local people is concerned.

The raids came as the culmination of weeks of careful surveys by investigators from the Greensboro office of the federal alcohol tax unit. T. E. Patton, of Charlotte, investigator in charge of the alcohol tax unit in North Carolina, and A. J. Littleton, assistant investigator in charge, were notified, in order that they might have part in direction and execution of the raiding projects.

Assisting Mr. Patton and Mr. Littleton were Investigator J. R. Brandon, in charge of the Greensboro office, and Investigators F. D. Lumpkin, J. B. Banks and C. S. Felts, who launched the original investigation; J. C. Fortner, Leonard Roup, J. T. Jones and L. J. Bishop. Approximately a dozen laborers were secured to assist in the destruction of the confiscated property.

The raiding was conducted in the Ingle Hollow section of Wilkes county, about 15 miles east of Wilkesboro. Having learned that extensive quantities of liquor on which no federal tax had been paid were being made in unregistered distilleries, the investigators, however, did not at first realize that they were about to put an end to such huge operations. Some idea of the immensity of the seizures may be gained from the calculation that federal taxes and penalties on the liquor seized would aggregate approximately $28,000.

The illicit activities were found to center near the home of Glenn Johnson. Johnson and his wife and their five children live in a residence containing eight rooms, but much of mountain liquor was stored in four of those rooms, in which were found 1,113 cases, 50 five-gallon cans, three 50-gallon barrels and a 15-gallon keg filled with corn whisky. As the officers approached Johnson ran and he has not yet been apprehended.

The work of destruction of the distilling equipment was accomplished Sunday by Investigators Brandon, Lumpkin, Felts, Fortner and Roup, with the aid of a group of laborers. Already the vast stores of liquor had been poured out and the automobile and sugar had been confiscated.

Investigations by the officers disclosed that the stills had been operated over a considerable period of time; runs had very recently been completed in two of them. It is quite evident that the liquor manufacturing industry in Wilkes has been struck a decidedly telling blow.

This photograph and clipping were released by news wire services following the 1935 raid on the Johnson home. The raid was reported as the largest inland seizure of illegal whiskey ever made in America. (Junior Johnson collection)

# CHAPTER TWO

Junior started driving his father's pickup truck when he was about eight or nine years old. At fourteen, he began delivering moonshine, even though he wasn't old enough to have a valid North Carolina driver's license.

"When the time came for me to get on the road, I was confident I could do anything anyone else could do," Junior says.

At the beginning, he didn't travel very far from home. Most of the time, he went to Yadkinville, about 20 miles away, where he had a regular customer.

"It was a good way to start because I could run on these little dirt roads late at night and stay off the main roads. That helped me learn pretty quick."

Junior's enterprise wasn't based solely on his father's operation. He also hauled moonshine for his older brothers. Eventually, most of his time was spent working for himself.

Junior's nemesis was Sid Carter of the North Carolina Highway Patrol. Carter was the only state patrolman in the area, so he knew everyone—especially Junior.

"He chased me, but he never caught me," Junior says. "However fast he was going at the time he was chasing me,

## "I just mashed the gas."

Above right: Junior poses in front of one of his first Sportsman Division race cars. He had started driving when he was eight or nine years old; at fourteen he began hauling moonshine even though he wasn't old enough to have a valid North Carolina driver's license. (Junior Johnson collection)

Opposite: One of the many cars Junior used for moonshining was a 1952 Ford, like this restored model. When he bought it new, Junior replaced the engine with a larger Cadillac engine for extra power. The car was so fast that Junior took it to Daytona Beach for a measured-mile exhibition in 1954. (Clay Call collection)

# "With the rear seat taken out, there was plenty of room in the back to stack cases of liquor," Junior says. "Of course, you packed 'em in the trunk, too.

that's what he'd charge me with—speeding, reckless driving, something like that—and I'd go down to court and they'd try me and, most times, take my driver's license.

Sometimes Sid Carter didn't try at all.

"He knew who I was, so all he had to do was go to the court, tell 'em Junior was actin' up again, and they would let me know they'd pulled my license and it wasn't no good any more," Junior says.

Moonshine-hauling cars, which needed heavy-duty suspensions, were substantially modified under their stock bodies.

"The first thing you did was take the motor out," Junior says. "You'd bore the thing, stroke the crank, port the heads and manifolds, change the camshaft—you put a high-performance camshaft in it—and most of the time you put Edelbrock or Offenhauser cylinder heads in it. And most of the good running motors had three carburetors on 'em."

The motor of choice was the Flathead Ford, but the 454-cubic-inch Cadillac engine was often substituted. As time went on and technology advanced, overhead-valve engines came into production; these were soon followed by even more powerful supercharged powerplants, which did away with the Flathead Ford.

"With the rear seat taken out, there was plenty of room in the back to stack cases of liquor," Junior says. "Of course, you packed 'em in the trunk, too. You kept the spare tire. You'd take it loose, but there was a way of repacking it behind the moonshine so extra cases could get in there."

Stacking cases was an art form. Fourteen would fit nicely in the back of a 1939 or 1940 Ford, and they were positioned so that the tops of the cases were 6 inches below the bottom of the window. That way they could not be seen by passing motorists or the law.

Two cases were stacked on the passenger-side floor, and two more were placed flat on top of them. They were adjusted to form a brace for the driver's body when he made hard, fast turns to the left. There were no seat belts. Twenty-two cases made a night's load. That amounted to 120 gallons of moonshine.

Customers were acquired by word of mouth, through acquaintances.

"Basically, you would have to rely on your customer. You would ask if the guy's buddy was honest, wasn't the law, would pay on time, so on and so forth," Junior says.

The demand for whiskey was so great that, by Junior's estimate, 700 people in Wilkes County were hauling moonshine. "I'd see 'em all night long," Junior remembers. "I'd meet several cars, and I knew who was driving. Of course, my brothers were in it, just like I was. Fred drove for me about all the time."

Junior got his first car, a 1936 Ford, at fourteen, but he wasn't old enough to register it, so he put the title in his older sister Ruth's name. He earned the money to buy the car by working in moonshining and helping his father and uncle at the sawmill. He had many cars during his bootlegging career and learned early on how to take care of them. "You maintained your cars like they do racecars today," Junior recalls. "You'd go air your tires up, wash the car, change the oil, grease it, and do everything you had to do to it to have it ready to go out at night."

Junior had scheduled rounds. He usually started out at 11 P.M. and tried to return by 6 or 7 A.M. He avoided deliveries during the day because he could be easily recognized and forced to run away or hide. It was too dangerous.

The moonshine network started at some small, hidden still and stretched across the counties and cities in every direction. Junior delivered to small cities like Boone, Concord, and Kannapolis. There were also bigger cities, such as High Point, Lexington, Salisbury, and Thomasville.

Revenue officer Terry Hall (left) and Surry County deputy sheriff Heber Mounce stand with a 160-gallon load of moonshine that was confiscated on its way out of Wilkes County in 1959. The trunk shows how haulers would rearrange the contents, such as the spare tire on the right, to fit the maximum amount of moonshine. (Terry Hall collection)

These coke-fired stills were discovered and photographed in the backwoods of Wilkes County during the 1950s. According to Junior, these types of stills were perhaps the most popular of the era. (Terry Hall collection)

Wilkes County revenue officer Sam Cabe (right) worked in the area chasing moonshiners for 30 years. Junior occasionally had run-ins with Cabe, but was never caught by him. In an Associated Press article from the 1970s, Cabe referred to Wilkes County as "the Siberia post" for revenuers, adding that he would search for moonshiners so deep into the woods and mountains that he'd find them using "hoot owls for chickens." (Terry Hall collection)

The moonshine Junior delivered and sold might be sold twice again before finally reaching the end customer. The first buyer would make his profit by reselling it to someone else, who then might take it to another bigger city like Charlotte and sell it there.

"You always left in plenty of time so you would get to where you told a guy you would be at a certain time in the morning, like one o'clock," Junior explains. "He would pay you for the moonshine, and that's when you would ask him when he needed another load. Say it was Monday night. He would probably tell you he needed another load on Wednesday night or Thursday night. I would go back and prepare to carry the next load to him at the specified time. It was just like you'd prepare for a regular job. Just like punching a clock at work."

A successful twenty-two-case haul meant a profit of $5 per case, or $110 per run. A quart mason jar of bootleg whiskey sold for about $1.25. It wasn't unusual for Junior to make $350 to $450 a night, which would equate to approximately $1,000 in today's economy. To earn that meant three or four runs per night, seven nights a week.

The car never lost its status as the vehicle of choice for moonshiners, but many of them began to use trucks to meet the increasing demand.

"We could take 150 cases on a ton-and-a-half truck, but it didn't stop there," Junior recalled. "It got up to a point a time or two that we were hauling tractor-trailer loads. That was 575 cases a load. That meant even more money if you got the job done."

Despite the heady profits, there were operating expenses that decreased moonshiners' income. They had to pay for ingredients like sugar and corn, and they had to maintain their cars. They were also hit with unplanned expenses. A car could be lost or confiscated. Stills could be blown up, perhaps as many as three or four a night.

"Basically, it was a good way to make a living, but it was a risky business," Junior says.

Robert Glenn Johnson went to prison four or five times, by Junior's count, for a total of ten years.

"The first time he went up for four or five years," Junior says. "Even if he got paroled, he served about a third of that time. And he got a couple of two-year sentences and two or three sentences of eighteen months each. Over a period of years, he spent a lot of time in prison."

"We had seen my father make money and have money for the family, and one way he did that was by moonshining," Junior says. "I asked myself more than once, 'What else could I do to make that much money?' There was nothing. So we continued to do it, even when my father was in prison."

It was so routine for the elder Johnson to be behind bars that the rest of the family had established a regimen to follow while he was gone. The brothers ran the moonshining operation while Lora Belle oversaw the farm. There were cattle, pigs, crops, and some liquor money at their disposal, so the Johnsons were never in danger of going without while the father was locked up.

But life was still difficult.

"It was harder when my father was gone," Junior says. "We just couldn't provide for ourselves the way my father had provided for us. We didn't starve or anything, but those were still some tough times when my father was in jail."

In all the years Junior hauled moonshine, as many as four times per night, seven days per week, month after month, year after year, Junior was never caught on the road by revenuers. They tried the usual roadblocks and stakeouts, and, even though there was a time or two they came close to nabbing him, he always got away.

It took more than driving skill and a powerful car to escape. For example, to beat the roadblocks, Junior

This still shows the extent moonshiners would go to hide their stills in remote areas of the Brushy Mountains in Wilkes County (right). Revenue officers discovered it amongst a dense patch of trees in 1966 and destroyed it with dynamite (far right). (Terry Hall collection)

sometimes employed a siren and a red light. "You could speed right toward that roadblock, and when they saw you comin', they figured you were the law and they'd move their cars right off the road," Junior says. "There were some surprised looks when you shot right by 'em."

Junior's father told him about another evasive maneuver, which was to drop oil onto a car's hot exhaust system to provide an instant smoke screen. This was done by rigging a small line from the oil pan to the exhaust.

"You could blend black and red pepper into the oil," Junior says, "and when it hit the exhaust, why, when the lawmen got a whiff of that in the smoke, it would be so bad many of 'em had to get to a hospital to get over the stinging in their eyes. Haulers used the pepper against lawmen they thought were smart-asses."

This is the patch worn by the North Carolina Board of Alcoholic Control. (Terry Hall collection)

Revenuers had a few tricks they used, too, although Junior never fell prey to them.

They would slick the roads with oil. They would also use a tire-shredding belt of spikes and nails. One agent would inform another via radio that the moonshine hauler was on the way, and the other agent would throw the belt on the road. A tire would blow out and the hauler would be nabbed.

"I never saw one of 'em, though," Junior says.

The closest Junior came to being collared on the road was when he was eighteen or nineteen years old. He'd been in the business as a hauler for four to five years and had begun to train aspiring bootleggers.

One night Junior and a trainee were going to Lexington, east of Wilkes County, but they first made a stop in Morganton to pick up the local liquor. Later, on the way to Lexington, Junior noticed he was running low on fuel. "I saw that we had only about four or five miles to go where we was taking the whiskey, so I kept going," Junior says.

Junior's customer had another man with him. What neither of them knew was that this man was working with the revenuers.

The plan was for Junior and his trainee to remain in the car. The customer got into the car, moving the trainee to the middle of the front seat. As Junior positioned the car to unload, the law pounced.

"So I just mashed the gas and headed down a dirt road, but they had it blocked," Junior says. "I didn't pay that no mind. I just went up around it, riding up a bank. I sped on, trying to get away from 'em as fast as I could. But there was a problem. I was running out of gas. I had to find someplace to get some gas or set the whiskey off, hide, or whatever I could do."

Junior told his trainee to get in the backseat, on top of the liquor, so it would be easier to drive.

Junior recalls: "I kept a-goin' and the guy sittin' beside me, the customer, got so scared he told me, 'Junior, if you stop, I'll pay you for this car and the load of liquor and everything. I don't care if they catch me. You're gonna kill every one of us.' The friend of mine layin' up on top of that liquor said, 'It don't make no difference what it takes, stop and let me out. If they take this car, I'll pay for it.' "

But Junior wasn't going to stop. The law was out of sight, and he figured he could get away.

He went on a bit and ducked behind a man's house. There wasn't anyone at home. Junior had found a place to hide. He noticed a farm tractor sitting out in the yard.

"So we sat there a few minutes and I got to thinking, 'I wonder if that tractor has any gas in it?' " Junior says. "So I got out of the car and headed toward the tractor, and I broke me off a little stick from a little tree and I stuck it in the gas tank. It was just plumb full of gas."

Junior's next problem was not having anything with which to siphon the gas.

"Back at that time," Junior says, "a 1940 Ford had a little rubber hose that they covered up with upholstery that ran all the way up and across the top of the door and back down again. It was insulation to keep the air out of the car. So I took me a knife, cut through the upholstery, got out that rubber hose, and used it to draw out the gas in the tractor."

"I got me about ten gallons. I took out some money, about twice what the gas was worth, and put it on the seat of that tractor with a rock on top of it. And I knew another person in Lexington who would take the liquor, so I took it to him and unloaded it."

Junior took the customer back to his house. The law had already been there. They figured that's where he would go.

"After, I got to thinking about it," Junior says. "You know that the moonshine business is pretty dangerous, but if you ride with a guy who offers to pay for the car and all the liquor if you let him out of the car—even if the law does catch him—you know he's pretty a-scared.

"But I was determined I wasn't going to give up my car."

Once, however, he gave it up to serve the law. In the mid-'50s, Junior was working a haul to Lenior with Gwyn Staley. After loading their cars, they headed back the way they had come. At the county line, they had to negotiate a sharp curve. As they did so, they noticed dirt and debris on the road.

"We locked 'em down and got stopped," Junior says. "We saw a car turned on its side off the road. Both of us jumped out of our cars and ran up to it, and we knew both of the guys in the car. One of them was the high sheriff."

Both of them, battered but otherwise uninjured, were dead drunk.

"They couldn't hardly stand up," Junior says.

Staley asked Junior just what were they going to do with a drunk lawman and an associate who, under normal circumstances, would have arrested both of them.

"I said, 'Well, I'll load one of 'em on top of the cases in my car, and the other one can ride with you,' " Junior recalls. "We agreed to do that. So we slid 'em both in our cars and we took 'em to the back of the courthouse and we let 'em both out. They were both skinned up and their car was tore up."

After dispatching the sheriff and his associate, Junior stopped at a filling station, refueled, and completed his delivery.

"Every once in a while after that, every time I'd see the sheriff, he'd kinda grin and say, 'You ain't been up the road lately, have you?' " Junior says. "It might have been close a time or two, but most of the chases was funny, especially to a younger person like me. But even so, you respected the men who were chasing you."

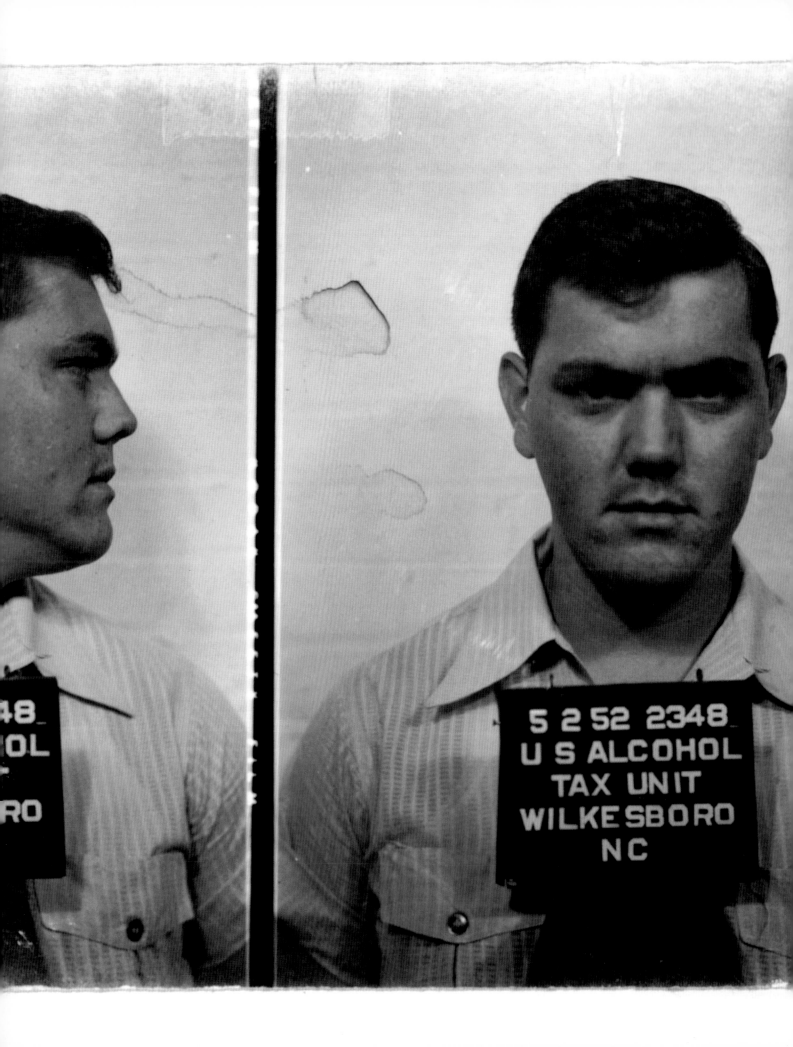

# CHAPTER THREE

Through the early 1950s, Junior remained deeply involved in his father's moonshining operation, and the chases continued. He often competed with revenuers and other lawmen in high-speed highway pursuits. This should have produced plentiful excitement for a young man who loved driving fast cars.

Yet Junior wanted more.

By 1952, NASCAR founder Big Bill France had built up his Grand National circuit and was taking stock car racing to a larger market. There were 33 races that season at such disparate locations as West Palm Beach, Florida; Canfield, Ohio; and Rochester, New York.

Junior yearned to test his driving talent and courage against the likes of Buck Baker, Tim Flock, Lee Petty, and Curtis Turner. In 1953 he got the chance.

Junior had a 1953 Olds Holiday to drive the Southern 500 on Labor Day at Darlington Raceway in South Carolina. He would make his Grand National debut on a track that, since it was built in 1950, has been rated NASCAR's toughest.

## "That put the brakes on me and racing."

Opposite: **In 1952 Junior was arrested in Wilkes County for hauling illegal liquor, but the charges were later dropped. Junior wanted to leave moonshining and concentrate on professional stock car racing, but the money in racing was not comparable. (Junior Johnson collection)**

Above right: **Big band leader Paul Whiteman became interested in racing during 1954 and was encouraged by Bill France to hire Junior as one of his drivers. The car was the No. 7 Cadillac, shown here to the left of a street Cadillac. The screen placed over the grille was to prevent clods of dirt from getting stuck in the radiator, causing the engine to overheat. (Daytona Racing Archives)**

The Delta 88 "Police Special" was specially made by Oldsmobile for law enforcement with optional heavy-duty suspension and uprated power. Ironically, this also made it ideal for hauling liquor. Junior bought a Police Special and says, "when we weren't using it to haul the race car, I was using it to haul liquor." This Oldsmobile publicity photo shows a Police Special with the usual siren and law enforcement markings, neither of which was on Junior's car. (Oldsmobile)

Junior qualified the No. 75 automobile for the twenty-sixth starting position in a fifty-nine-car field. He completed 222 of the 364 laps on the treacherous, egg-shaped layout before being involved in a crash along the backstretch. He finished thirty-eighth in the event won by Baker in an Olds 88. Junior's purse was only $110, a paltry amount considering the risk involved. Nevertheless, he loved what he had experienced and knew that he would be coming back for a lot more.

However, the 1954 season held only four starts at the Grand National level for Junior. Three of these came in a car owned by Paul Whiteman, the leader of one of America's most popular big bands. The car was a Cadillac.

"Bill France got me and Whiteman together," recalled Junior. "They were very good friends, and Bill was encouraging Whiteman to get into racing.

"Whiteman was very famous, but he was what I call a 'regular ol' Joe.' I got along good with him.

"The Cadillacs back then, of course, were big, heavy cars. For NASCAR, as it was at that time, the Cadillac made a pretty good racecar. Mine ran fairly well, but I didn't finish real good the three times we ran."

Junior's best showing in the Caddy was a fifteenth at Langhorne (Pennsylvania) Speedway in a 250-miler on September 26, 1954.

In 1955 Junior returned to his Wilkes County roots to form the team that would first make him a winner at the Grand National level.

"Me and two local businessmen, Carl Buchanan and Jim Lowe, got a deal going," remembers Junior.

They had been business associates for years, as Junior had bought cars from Lowe. Lowe suggested he and Junior build a car for NASCAR competition and see what they could do.

For a startup, it was a good race team. Lowe's affiliation with Oldsmobile meant that the fledgling operation would get some assistance from General Motors. Lowe also had the benefit of some good mechanics at his dealership. Everything seemed in place, so Junior, who didn't have to pull a dime out of his pocket, agreed to be the driver.

"It was a deal where you didn't have to put up any money to drive for somebody," Junior says. "It was a deal where you just showed up at the racetrack with your helmet. You didn't have to worry about getting locked up for what you were doing to make money."

The team had a Delta 88 and Oldsmobile donated parts and pieces. Because of Oldsmobile's generosity, Junior bought a Delta 88 to haul liquor. The car was called a "Police Special" because of its optional heavy-duty suspension and uprated power, and was designed for use by law enforcement officials. "We used it to haul the racecar all around the place," Junior says. "And when we weren't using it to haul the racecar, I was using it to haul liquor."

The inaugural triumph came on May 7, 1955, at Hickory Speedway in North Carolina. Junior qualified second, sharing the front row for the start with Tim Flock, who won the pole on the four-tenths-mile dirt track at 67.478 MPH in a Chrysler fielded by the powerful Carl Kiekhaefer–owned team. Johnson and Flock battled so hard that Junior twice spun out while leading. Each time, Junior charged back to regain the lead. He forged ahead for keeps on the 172nd of 200 laps in the 80-mile race.

"Kiekhaefer was so mad I thought he was goin' to blow a gasket," says Junior, grinning with pleasure at the memory. "He filed a protest about the outcome with NASCAR almost the minute the race was over. Kiekhaefer was yelling, 'No one can outrun my cars! No one can outrun my cars!' I got tired of hearing it, and I said to him,

Junior stands next to the Whiteman Cadillac that he drove with Gwyn Staley. Up to that point Junior had accomplished most of his success at the Sportsman level, and had not competed regularly in Grand National racing. Nevertheless, Whiteman chose him because of his reputation as a win-or-crash-trying driver. Notice the misspelling of Junior's name on the car and the common plumbing pipe and elbow joint that make up the roll bar. (Daytona Racing Archives)

**Right:** Friends and fellow racers Bob Welborn (left) and Glen Wood (middle) sit with Junior at North Wilkesboro Speedway before a 1956 Sportsman Division race. Wood drove the Grand National circuit from 1953 through 1964 before gaining greater fame as a team owner. (Mike Staley collection)

**Opposite:** Junior stands in front of his brand-new 1956 Pontiac, sponsored by Brushy Mountain Motors, before a 39-lap race at the Daytona Beach and Road Course in 1956. It was only the second time Junior had competed at Daytona. (Mike Staley collection)

'That's a bunch of shit, 'cause I just did.' NASCAR started inspecting our car. They took out the transmission, crankshaft, and camshaft. Kiekhaefer yelled, 'Give me that camshaft!' and he grabbed it. I told him, 'I didn't know you was an inspector.'

"Nothing was illegal. Then they couldn't get the car put back together. NASCAR made Kiekhaefer pay to fix it. Really tickled me."

The Hickory, North Carolina, race, the season's twelfth, launched Junior on a tear. He won race No. 17 at Raleigh, No. 19 at New Oxford, Pennsylvania, and No. 21 at Fonda, New York. In each event Flock was the runner-up.

Six weeks later, Junior scored his fifth and final victory of 1955 in a race at Altamont, New York. The race ended prematurely when a single-car crash destroyed a stretch of fence fronting the grandstand.

Although often running on tracks he'd never seen before, Junior compiled a remarkable record in what amounted to his rookie season. In all but his first triumph during the season, Junior finished a lap or more ahead of the runner-up. In addition to the victories, he posted seven other top-five finishes and eighteen top tens in his thirty-six starts, finishing sixth in the point standings.

"It seems incredible now, 'cause we ran that whole season with just one car," says Junior. "We worked on it almost constantly between races, pulling over at service stations, little ol' garages, anywhere we could find. We even worked on it in the parking lots at the motels where we stayed."

He was also beating the best of the best, drivers such as Ralph Moody, Marvin Panch, Edward Glenn "Fireball" Roberts, Curtis Turner, and Joe Weatherly, all of whom were backed by the deep pockets of Ford.

Although the Rookie of the Year award didn't exist for newcomers in 1955, fans quickly discerned that Johnson, just twenty-four, was something very special. His charging, full-bore, give-no-quarter style enthralled spectators who began overflowing the grandstands to watch the daredevil liquor-hauler drive.

The fans tagged Junior "The Wilkes County Wild Man" and "The Ronda Roadrunner."

When 1955 came to a close, Junior realized racing could be good for him financially, especially if he could win his share of races against the factory teams. That could lead to a factory ride for himself.

In 1956, he signed a contract with Ford, opting for the Detroit giant over an offer from Kiekhaefer.

But despite Junior's success at racing, he remained in the moonshine business. It was like a bad habit. Like a smoker fighting to quit, Junior had to have one last drag. And then another.

"It had gotten so big, and I had put so much into it, it just wasn't that easy to walk away," Junior says. "I was doing it less and less. But I still wasn't completely out of it. It was gonna take time."

Less than three weeks after he signed the contract with Ford, Junior paid for his bad habit.

Junior came home from a midsummer race at New Oxford, Pennsylvania, which he had won. It was a night race that started at 8 on Sunday, and it was in the dark hours of Monday morning that he returned. Robert Glenn met his son and asked him to fire up the still. It was the ideal time to set fire to the wood, because the darkness would hide the smoke.

"I did what any boy would do," Junior says. "I did what my daddy asked me to do."

Junior didn't know he was being watched. The revenuers had found the Johnson still, or someone had told them where it was, and they had the area staked out.

This police mugshot was taken after Junior's arrest at the Johnson home on June 2, 1956. It was the only time Junior was found guilty of moonshining and was forced to serve time in prison. At the time of the booking, Junior had been hauling moonshine for 10 years. He was 24. (Junior Johnson collection)

**Below:** After Junior was ambushed at his father's still and tried to escape, this warrant was issued for Junior and his father's arrest. (Nigel Kinrade)

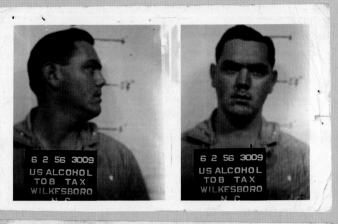

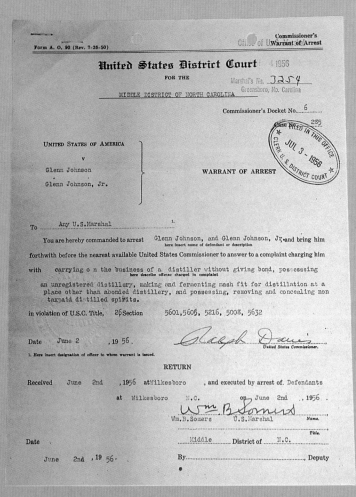

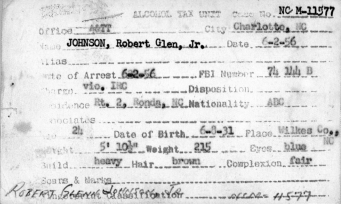

"They had been trying to catch me for years, and they focused on me totally when they saw it was me who had come in to fire up that still," Junior says. "My daddy and two brothers, Fred and L.P., and an uncle of mine were coming in to run the still for the rest of the day."

As he fired the still, Junior heard his father, brothers, and uncle approaching with the equipment needed for the day's work. He could see the beams of their flashlights within 200 to 300 yards of the still.

Coke, a form of coal that burned much hotter, was used to fire up the still. As Junior took a shovel of coke to throw into the burner, he looked over his right shoulder.

"I saw a guy named John West," Junior says. "At the time, he was running the revenue service in Wilkes County. He was standing on a box, just fixin' to jump right on top of my back.

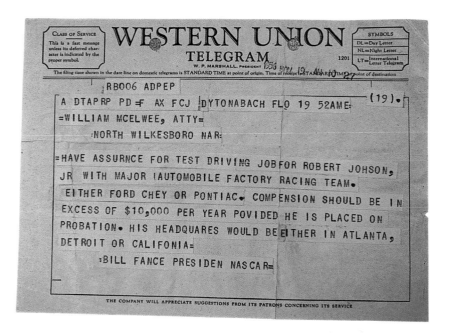

"When I seen him, I knew he was fixin' to jump on me. So I took the coke, shovel, and everything and threw it in his face as he came toward me. Then I took off."

It may have seemed foolish to run through the woods in the dark, but Junior had no choice. If he could get away, it would make it more difficult to prove he was ever on the property.

Plus, he had the advantage of knowing the terrain. Some distance away, below the still, there was a fence with a gate. Junior knew the gate was open because cows had been coming and going at their leisure. If he could hit that open gate on a dead run, his chances for getting away were good.

"I knew I had to hit that gate, because if I didn't, I was caught," Junior says. "I hadn't had a chance to gain much ground on the guy who was chasin' me. He was a very physical type, an athletic-type person. It wasn't John West. When I gave him that shovelful of coke, that was the end of him."

Junior missed the gate. He ran directly into a barbed-wire fence. He struggled hard to escape the sharp barbs that tore his clothes and flesh. By the time he did, West's associate was upon him.

"He jumped on my back and pinned me down," Junior says.

Meanwhile, West had gone to the Johnson house, thinking Junior would return. Instead, he found Robert Glenn Johnson and told him he knew it was his son at the still who had thrown the coke in his face, and if he wasn't caught that night, he might as well turn himself in.

"That put the brakes on me and racing," Junior says.

In November 1956, Junior went to federal court in North Wilkesboro. It was a busy court because of the amount of moonshining cases tried there. Judge Johnson Hayes, a tough disciplinarian on moonshiners, was presid-

ing, and when he saw Junior and his father, charged with manufacturing illegal whiskey, standing before him, he must have felt a surge of glee.

"I tried every way I could to work with the judge, to get out of it any way I could," Junior says. He thought he might be able to pay a fine, but that wasn't likely.

"Hayes was tough on us because my father was one of the largest moonshiners in the area," Junior says. "He was supposed to be the kingpin. So Hayes gave my father two to three years. And he gave me two years."

Junior went to federal prison in Chillocothe, Ohio. His life there was routine. There was no sense fighting the system or testing the rules. Besides, it wasn't in his nature. In his society, he wasn't a criminal. He was a hard-working man in a profession that, unfortunately, was against the law.

He worked the prison's farm detail and maintained farm machinery, something he had been doing at home nearly all his life. He was so adept at it he taught other inmates so they could work on farms when they were released. He got help from a handful of inmates from Wilkes County who knew farming as well as he did.

The prison wasn't considered a maximum-security unit, but Junior recalls there were some inmates who had been sentenced to life. Many had gotten in trouble while in the Army, committing crimes as serious as rape and murder. Junior avoided them.

"The only thing I was interested in was gettin' out of there," Junior says. "That meant walking the line and stayin' out of everyone's way. So that's what I did."

Eleven months and three days after the grim moment he walked through the prison gates, he was paroled. He went home and started racing again.

He also went back to moonshining.

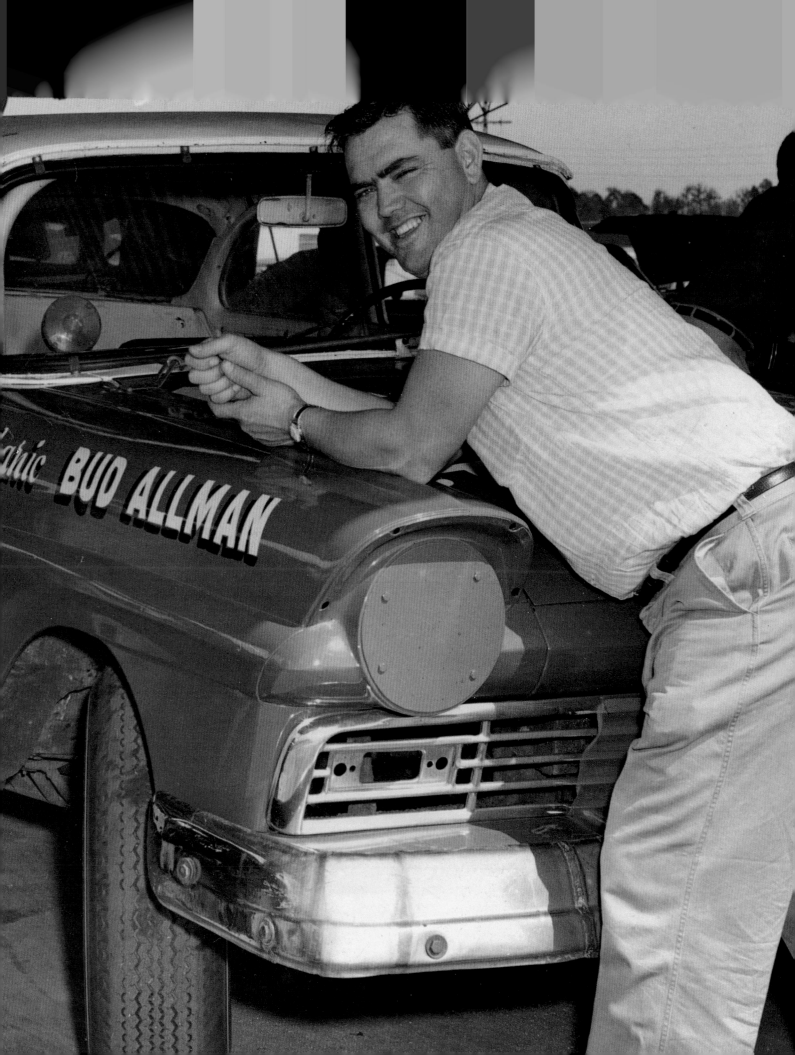

# CHAPTER FOUR

Because of his troubles with the law, Junior ran only thirteen races in 1956 and one in 1957, posting just one top-ten finish.

Ironically, the latter was achieved in a Dodge fielded by Kiekhaefer.

Junior was "just present as a spectator" at the Charlotte Fairgrounds when Kiekhaefer asked him to drive a Dodge he'd brought along with his regular Chryslers.

"Kiekhaefer called for his drivers to gather around him," says Junior. "He had five matches in his hand of varying lengths. He told us to draw a match each. Whoever got the shortest match was to finish first; whoever got the longest was to finish fifth. The others were to place in between in the order dictated by the length of their match."

Junior got the second shortest match.

"I didn't like it," Junior says, "but I was going along with Carl's program as the race got started. Then, whoever drew what was supposed to be fifth place came by and blowed my doors off. Then another of 'em came by. I said to myself, 'The hell with this—I'm going to race!' So I got up there to runnin' with 'em."

Even though Kiekhaefer's script for the race was disregarded, Junior wound up finishing second to Kiekhaefer regular Speedy Thompson. Buck Baker, also driving for

## "I never looked back."

Above right: Car owner Carl Kiekhaefer, pictured with regular drivers Herb Thomas, Buck Baker, and Speedy Thompson, asked Junior to drive for him at Charlotte Speedway in 1956. It was the only race he drove for Kiekhaefer. (Daytona Racing Archives)

Opposite: Junior was in good spirits next to the Paul Spaulding-owned and Bud Allman-prepared 1958 Ford before a race. It was Junior's first ride after serving eleven months in federal prison in Chillocothe, Ohio. (Mike Staley collection)

Junior returned to racing with a vengeance in 1958, tearing up the track with the same abandon he had before his arrest. He finished the year with six victories and was eighth in the championship standings, driving behind the wheel of Paul Spaulding's No. 11 1957 Ford. (Daytona Racing Archives)

Kiekhaefer, was third. "After the race, Kiekhaefer told me that he didn't need me anymore," continues Junior. "I told him that was fine with me, 'cause I'd rather beat him than run for him. Carl was awful ornery at times, but I liked him, and we remained friends through the years."

It was in 1958 that Wilkes County saw Junior come home. While Junior was stuck in jail the year before, Ford pulled out of stock car racing and sold off its cars. A man named Paul Spaulding from Syracuse, New York, bought a 1957 Ford from the powerhouse Holman-Moody team in Charlotte, North Carolina. Mechanic Bud Allman of Conover, North Carolina, maintained the car at his shop.

When Allman learned Junior had returned, he contacted him and asked if he wanted to drive the car. Junior said yes, made the deal, and drove his first race as an ex-con in Columbia, South Carolina.

On May 18, in a race at North Wilkesboro Speedway, Junior showed his immense driving talent hadn't diminished despite his time away. He was leading by a half-lap when he went into the third turn too hard, careened over an embankment that served as a retaining barrier, sliced through a patch of weeds, and came back on the track still ahead of the second place car, driven by Marvin Panch. Junior held on to win. A crowd estimated at 6,000 went wild at the sight of the local hero pulling off such a feat.

"Back then, the newly paved tracks seemed to tear up pretty easily," Junior says. "I got into the loose stuff, or pieces of asphalt 'marbles,' and went over that 4-foot high bank. I never touched the brakes. I knew the only chance I had was to keep my speed up to get through those weeds and back over that bank, so that's what I did." It was Junior's first victory in almost three years and served notice of things to come.

Junior won three times in June 1958. He scored at Columbia, then took a weekend doubleheader during the grand opening of a one-third-mile track at Bradford, Pennsylvania. He won the fall race at North Wilkesboro.

As Junior battled for the lead at North Wilkesboro, a fan sitting in the grandstand near the first turn became angered by the driving of one of Junior's rivals. Track promoter Enoch Staley remembered it this way: "The next lap that guy racing Junior so hard came around the track I saw something sail out of the stands and over the fence right in front of his car. It hit the track and broke into a thousand pieces. It was a quart-sized fruit jar filled with white liquor. We were strong against anything being thrown on the track, but this was sort of amusing because of what the object happened to be. I couldn't imagine a man getting so mad he'd throw away a quart of good moonshine."

Junior saw the jar flying toward his challenger's car.

"The next few laps around I'd glance into the stands and I saw that the law had come to the scene and was trying to arrest the guy," says Junior with a smile. "There was a pretty lively scuffle going on 'til the deputies got him handcuffed and took him off."

And who was the culprit? Staley took delight in saying, "Junior didn't tell the rest of the story. The fan that got taken to jail was a feller named Ernest Money. He was Junior's uncle."

The biggest triumph of Junior's career to that point came on October 26, 1958, when he won at Atlanta's Lakewood Speedway, a one-mile dirt track that was among the best-known layouts in Dixie. Junior took the lead with fifteen laps to go from the sport's brightest star at the time, Fireball Roberts.

"That win in Atlanta ranks way up among my favorites," Junior says. "This is on account of where it was and who I

This overhead shot of North Wilkesboro shows the track during its transformation from a dirt track to an asphalt speedway in 1957. In the background beyond the track is U.S. Highway 421, the main road Junior used to haul moonshine out of Wilkes County. (Mike Staley collection)

Judge Edwin M. Stanley presided over the 1959 Johnson trial for alleged moonshining activities, and his hand-written notes show behind-the-scenes access to the Johnson family's whiskey hauling. Page two details the plaintiff's description of the Johnson home and moonshine operation. Page nine details a conversation between L.P. and Junior, as well as what appears to be Junior's personal testimony. "Had Darlington race on mind," refers to the 1958 Southern 500 on September 1, where Junior finished eleventh. (Nigel Kinrade)

The details of the revenuer raids that led to the Johnson family arrests in September 1958 are reported in this *Charlotte Observer* story.

# Top-Ranking Race Driver Among Alleged Bootleggers

**By KEN CLARK**
Observer Staff Writer

WILKESBORO — The latest Wilkes County moonshine crackdown reached a successful climax Thursday with the arrest of five more people, including one of the top-ranked stock car racers in the country and his mother.

This brought to 10 the number arrested in a two-day period.

Federal and state liquor officers Thursday arrested Wes Welborn of Rt. 2, Ronda, and Richard Chambers and Dallas Hudspath, both of Rt. 1, Cycle. Both were charged with selling non-tax-paid whisky.

Junior Johnson, ranked among the five top NASCAR race drivers in the nation, surrendered voluntarily with his mother Thursday morning. Two of his brothers, L. P. and Fred Johnson, were arrested Wednesday.

Also picked up Wednesday were Jake Mathis and James William (Dickie) Pardue, both of Rt. 2, Ronda, and Chester Coffey of Rt. 3, North Wilkesboro. Mathis and Pardue were arrested after an all-night wait in Iredell County and Coffey was seized at his home.

All 10 persons are now out on bond awaiting hearings Oct. 3.

Jubilant ATTU officials said late Thursday that some of the men arrested were the "top violators" in the Wilkes area, and said the arrests would knock a big dent in liquor traffic.

And while the arrests were being made another group of 17 federal and state officers finished a four-day "saturation" program during which they walked out every branch in the county and destroyed 16 stills.

Officers went to the home of Junior Johnson Wednesday to arrest L. P., Fred Johnson and their mother. The officers found more whisky in the home.

One of the last moonshine cars that Junior drove was a 1959 Dodge similar to this restored model. Junior used the Dodge because of its strong motor and enhanced power. "There were two four-barrel carburetors on the engine," Junior says. (Clay Call Collection)

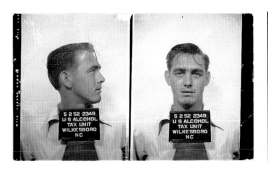   

Fred (left) and L.P. (middle) Johnson were arrested with Junior in 1952 for moonshining violations, but only L.P. and Fred were convicted. Records at the Alcohol and Tax Division in Charlotte show that between 1942 and 1958 the Johnson family committed twenty illegal liquor violations.

Junior's mother, Lora Belle (right), was arrested along with Junior, L.P., and Fred for making and distributing moonshine in 1958. Note that the image on the left is a double exposure. Junior's head-on mugshot is superimposed on Lora Belle's profile, and the number eight is superimposed over Lora Belle's case number in the upper right-hand corner of the identification sign. (Junior Johnson collection)

beat. After the race, most of the drivers and crews went back to the motel where practically all the racin' people stayed and we gathered to have some drinks. Fireball got to talkin' and said, 'There ain't no damn way anybody could drive a car like Junior did and not wreck.' I felt it was a heck of a compliment. I don't want to sound like I'm braggin', but when a car was really set up right, I could do some awesome things with it."

In all, Junior notched six victories in twenty-seven starts, a dozen top-five finishes, sixteen top tens, $13,808 in winnings, and eighth place in the point standings.

But Junior could not shake the moonshining habit. Records at the Alcohol and Tobacco Tax Division in Charlotte, which go back only to 1942, reveal that twenty violations or alleged violations had been committed by Johnson family members over sixteen years.

"I knew that racing was a better way of life," Junior says. "I could work four or five hours a week and not have to go to jail. That was the most important thing. I started looking at [racing full-time] real hard in 1958 when I got out. I started planning to do it."

But that planning took two years. And during those two years, Junior continued to haul whiskey, racing when he could.

"It was the family business and I had a lot invested in it in terms of doing the work," Junior says. "I could have walked away real quick like, but what would that have meant for my family? When I made money from moonshine, it was their money, too. How could I just cut off their money? So it took time to make slow changes, so, basically, we could reach a point where we all could get out of it."

The changes were too slow. In September of 1958, Junior, his brothers L.P. and Fred, and—remarkably—his mother Lora Belle, were charged with whiskey violations. Robert Glenn Johnson was not charged. He was already

in prison, less than a month away from completing a three-year term.

When the trial began in May of 1959, Junior's defense was that he could not possibly have been hauling illegal whiskey during the course of 1958 because he was competing on the NASCAR Grand National circuit.

Of course, this wasn't exactly true because Junior had been racing by day and hauling by night for years. But he had the support to make it work.

Paul Spaulding, a witness for the defense, said Junior had been testing and racing cars for him and had competed in nearly twenty races along the eastern seaboard. So he could not have been involved in the operation of the two stills agents found on the Johnson property, nor been around to complete undercover sales.

John Bruner, NASCAR's field manager, produced seventeen copies of the NASCAR bulletin that corroborated Spaulding's testimony.

Joe Epton, then the manager of Raleigh Speedway and later NASCAR's chief scorer, said Johnson was in Raleigh on the night of July 2, 1958, the night agents destroyed a huge still less than a mile from the Johnson home.

A Wilkes County native, Mrs. L.P. Privette, said another still that was found in October of 1958 was on her property and not the Johnsons'.

And finally, another Wilkes County native, Hubert Roberts, said he helped survey the area where the still was found in July and that in his opinion, the road on which the still was located was used by the general public, not just the Johnsons.

L.P. pleaded guilty to the charges and was given a one-year sentence on one count of whiskey violations, another two-year sentence to run concurrently with the first, and a three-year sentence to be served at the end of the two-year sentence. All this was boiled down to a

# Moonshine Activities Charged

**By KEN CLARK**
Observer Staff Writer

NORTH WILKESBORO — One of America's top-ranked race drivers, his mother and two brothers are on trial in the U. S. Middle District Court here on charges of conspiracy and manufacturing and selling white whiskey.

Junior Johnson of Ronda is currently ranked sixth in the NASCAR Grand National Racing Circuit. He, his mother, Mrs. Robert Glenn Johnson, and brothers Fred and L. P. Johnson were arrested last fall.

Two more Wilkes County men, James Franklin Ashley and Albert Ralph Grey of Cycle, are included in the charges.

A jury of eight men and one woman was chosen Monday. Both sides agreed on a nine-man jury after the list of potential jurors ran out.

Federal Judge Edwin M. Stanley is presiding.

The government is attempting to prove that the Johnsons, Ashley and Grey worked together in manufacturing, transporting and selling moonshine whisky last summer and fall.

Federal Alcohol and Tobacco Tax Division (ATTD) Agent David Edmiston, the first government witness, was on the stand over four hours Monday and Tuesday.

Edmiston testified that on July 2, 1958 he helped destroy a monstrous still on the Johnson farm in the Ingle Hollow section of Wilkes County.

He said the only road to the still led past the front door of the Johnson home, and that the road was partially concealed by a pile of wood.

**Left:** This *Charlotte Observer* story covers the 1959 moonshining trial that eventually found Junior innocent, but sentenced his brothers to prison terms. Lora Belle received a suspended sentence. (Junior Johnson collection)

**Opposite:** Junior was often found sleeping at racetracks before competition, the result of his late nights hauling moonshine. Here he naps at Darlington before the 1960 Southern 500. In the race Junior's engine failed after only 17 laps, which took him out of contention. He finished forty-seventh. (Don Hunter)

suspension of the three-year term and probation for five years. L.P. had to serve two years.

Fred Johnson was sentenced to thirty months in jail and fined $5,000.

After seeing evidence that Junior was indeed racing at the time of the raid, the nine-man jury found Junior innocent of all charges.

Lora Belle Johnson was fined $7,500 and given an eighteen-month suspended sentence for possessing and selling moonshine.

Records show that the family paid the fines. Moonshining provided the necessary funds.

The 1959 season was virtually a carbon copy of 1958 for the Johnson/Spaulding team. Junior won five of his twenty-seven starts, posted fourteen top fives and fifteen top tens, finished eleventh in points, and earned $9,674. Three of the victories are especially memorable.

On March 29 Junior edged out Curtis Turner, a colorful character whose background and driving style mirrored Junior's, by three seconds in a 100-miler at Wilson, North Carolina. A few minutes before the race was to begin, the main grandstand caught fire. The wooden structure was consumed by the blaze in minutes, but there were no injuries. Fans were directed to the backstretch, where they watched from a small bleacher or stood.

Back in home territory on May 2 for a race at Hickory, Junior flipped his Ford during practice. The car landed on its wheels.

"It's just skinned up a little bit," he said, shrugging off the accident.

Junior then won the pole and the race. Fans were awestruck.

On June 13 in a 100-mile event at Greenville-Pickens Speedway in South Carolina, a charging Junior quickly lapped the twenty-four other drivers in the field. Most competitors then would have eased off the throttle and coasted to the checkered flag.

Not Junior. He lapped everyone a second time.

The Wild Man continued his wild ride at Darlington later that year during preparation for the Southern 500.

"Norris Friel, NASCAR's head technical man at that time, made us change the rear end on our car," says Junior. "I was runnin' pretty hard in practice and going into the third turn, an axle broke as a result of the changes and the right rear tire fell off. The car took off just like an airplane and sailed over the rail and out of the track.

"It hit on its nose and basically tore apart. The motor and transmission came out as the car turned somersaults. When it finally came to a stop, about all that was left was the body of the car.

"The wreck jarred me so hard where the seatbelt was around my body that it hurt my back. But through the whole accident I never lost consciousness.

"I guess it looked a lot worse than it was for me physically. I was held overnight in a hospital at Florence [South Carolina]. I went back to the track and started the race in a T-bird.

"It was a bad wreck, but it didn't make me think about maybe slowing down. I knew it wouldn't have happened if that axle hadn't broken."

Junior was often spotted asleep in the garage areas, even napping sometimes on the hood of his race car. "Some people thought I was sleeping 'cause I was lazy," says Junior. "The truth is I was probably asleep because I had hauled liquor all night."

By 1960, Junior's continued moonshining had so frustrated the law that bounties from $5,000 to $10,000 had been placed on his head, payable to anyone who could help bring Wilkes County's most notorious moonshiner to justice.

A man would kill for that kind of money, and Junior knew it.

"It was just a matter of time, knowing the people I was dealing with and the way it worked," Junior says. "I had cut back on moonshining. I wasn't doing it nearly as much as I had, so the odds of catching me had dropped. I just wasn't on the road as much as I used to be. Racing still hadn't given me the kind of deal I felt I needed to leave it permanently. Still, if someone wanted to set me up, he could, and he wouldn't even have to give his name. He could put my hind end back in jail."

So Junior, now twenty-nine years old, a moonshiner for fifteen years and a prisoner for eleven months and three days, left the bootlegging business.

"I got out of it. And I never looked back," Junior says.

# CHAPTER FIVE

Even though Junior had won regularly and spectacularly for Paul Spaulding, the car owner decided to quit racing in 1960.

As the start of the season neared, Junior had no ride.

Then came a call from Ray Fox, a highly respected car builder/engineer/crew chief based in Daytona Beach, Florida. He had a Chevrolet with sponsorship from John Masoni through the Daytona Beach Kennel Club, the greyhound racing track Masoni owned near the first turn of the sprawling speedway. Fox needed a driver. Was Junior interested?

"It was essentially a spur-of-the-moment deal," recalls Fox. "The guy from the dog track came to me only eight days before the Daytona 500 and said very emphatically that he wanted a car in the race. I told him there was no way I could do it in that little bit of time. The guy, Masoni, left, but he returned the next day with a surprising offer.

"Masoni said to me, 'Whatever you charge to build and field racecars, I'll double it.' I thought about it and agonized about what to do. I finally said, 'Well, maybe I can hunt up enough guys to help me get it done.' I got the guys to my shop, put them to work, and phoned Junior."

"I liked Ray, so I told him I'd come down and see what we could do," says Junior. "It appeared that Pontiac had the

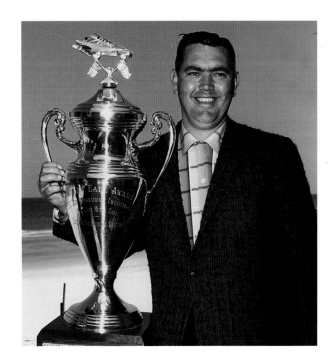

## "The car would draft like Jack the Bear."

**"They couldn't shake me. I knew then I was right about the air creating a situation—a slip-stream type of thing—in which a slower car could keep up with a much faster one. I saw this gave me a chance to win the race."**

best racecar, and several good drivers were in 'em, including Fireball and Paul Goldsmith. I knew it was going to be a challenge."

As he expected, the Pontiacs were up to 30 MPH faster than Junior in practice. And they stayed faster in time trials.

"I about decided that I was wasting my time," says Junior. "I was ready to come home. I didn't want to stay down there in Daytona and watch the Pontiacs lap me about every ten or eleven laps. I had no enthusiasm for it."

"Oh, hell, we were very slow," agrees Fox. "We only had a little 348-cubic-inch engine. The Pontiac engine was much better. I knew that. I was aware of the situation. On top of being outpowered, our car was a year old—it was a '59 model. The only reason I was in the race was because of the guy from the dog track making it so worth my while."

Junior hinted for Fox to get another driver. However, Fox demurred, vowing to improve his car's speed. After a series of adjustments, Junior decided to try and run along with a top Pontiac in practice.

"Cotton Owens came by and I got behind him. Right on his rear bumper. And I stayed right there! We came back to the garage and Cotton walked over to me. 'Boy, you've sure got that thing to running,' Cotton said. What he didn't know was that I had discovered the aerodynamic draft at Daytona. Even Ray thought we were faster due to him somehow fixing the car.

"I wanted to be sure of what I'd hit on, so I went back out to practice alone. The car was still the same—pretty slow.

"So I came onto pit road and sat there waitin' for some Pontiacs to come by. I got in with them on the track. And I stayed up.

"They couldn't shake me. I knew then I was right about the air creating a situation—a slipstream type of thing—in which a slower car could keep up with a much faster one. I saw this gave me a chance to win the race."

Junior started thirteenth in a 100-mile preliminary event on the sprawling Daytona speedway, which had opened in 1959. He finished fifth behind the Pontiacs of Roberts and Owens and the Fords driven by Fred Lorenzen and Joe Weatherly. This result gave Junior the ninth starting position for the second Daytona 500. "Once the race started, I got to the Pontiacs ahead of me as fast as I could," continued Junior. "From then on I did everything the Pontiac drivers did. If they pitted, I pitted."

"I knew that while our Chevrolet wouldn't run all that fast by itself on the track, the car would draft like Jack the Bear," says Fox. "And Junior had found out how to do that better than anyone. I knew this gave us a chance to win the race if Junior stayed around."

Various problems began taking a toll on the Pontiacs, sending them to the garage. Only the Pontiac of Bobby Johns remained competitive, and Junior had track position on him. However, the lapped Pontiac of Jack Smith gave Johns a tow and he passed Junior for the lead on the 170th lap of the race's 200.

"Then, coming off the second turn with ten laps to go, one of the damnedest things happened I ever saw on a racetrack," Junior recalls. "The back glass popped out of Bobby's car and flew into the air. I think our speed and the traffic circumstances combined to create a vacuum that sucked that back glass right out. The sudden change in the airflow around Bobby's car caused him to spin into the grass along the backstretch. By the time he got straightened out and back on the asphalt I was long gone."

"It came without warning," says Johns. "One second I'm racing along there in front knowing I can outrun Junior

pretty easily and the next second I'm spinning around and Junior is going by me."

Junior swept to the checkered flag 23 seconds ahead of Johns, who recovered to finish as the runner-up.

The father-son duo of Lee and Richard Petty placed third and fourth, respectively, in their Plymouths, and were the only other drivers to complete all 200 laps.

The immensely popular victory was the biggest of Junior's great career.

"I look back and it still amazes me that we won," he says. "The Chevy motor was sorry for racing at that time. The valves would come out and it wouldn't turn a lot of RPM. We had to run it at 7,500 RPMs that whole race just to keep up, so it's a wonder the motor lasted.

"On top of this, the 500 that year was filled with wrecks, and I was very, very close to several of them. I

At Charlotte, little-known Joe Lee Johnson (89) drops low to pass Tom Pistone (59) and pull away from Junior (27). The track was in such bad condition that drivers attached shields to the hood of their cars to deflect kicked-up asphalt. Joe Lee Johnson went on to victory in the event, which was only his second career win. (Don Hunter)

remember one guy wrecked along the backstretch in front of me and the engine came out of his car. I went into the grass and almost into the lake in the infield to miss that mess. I was within two or three feet of being involved in other big wrecks."

The crashes exacted such a toll on the sixty-eight cars in the race that NASCAR was forced to cancel the next two races. Most observers traced the trouble to drivers being unaccustomed to the scorching speeds at the 2.5-mile, high-banked Daytona track.

"I guess that's probably the reason a lot of 'em wrecked, but the speed wasn't any problem to me," Junior says. "See, my liquor-hauling cars were light and they had big engines that had been bored and stroked, and carried three or even four carburetors. Some of the engines had superchargers. So in running a racecar at Daytona it's not like I was sitting down in something I wasn't used to. We were going about 150 miles an hour at Daytona. I had run cars faster than that on the highway." Junior smiles and shakes his head. "I had run 'em so fast on the highway sometimes that the road ahead looked only a foot wide."

Among the races Junior ran in 1960 was the inaugural World 600 at Charlotte Motor Speedway. Controversy swirled around the facility being developed by Curtis Turner and local auto dealer Bruton Smith from the beginning. There were construction delays and a shortage of funds. Turner had so many hassles with contractors that he began toting a pistol. The 600 was scheduled for May 29, but the 1.5-mile track wasn't ready. The race was rescheduled for June 19. Paving work on the racing surface continued right into race week.

"The asphalt didn't have time to 'cure,' " recalls Junior. "So it was a major mess at Charlotte. The track tore apart in chunks. The situation demanded that they go on with the show. So everyone outfitted their cars with heavy grilles to keep big pieces of asphalt from penetrating the radiators and damaging the engines. Some teams even put deflectors on the hoods to keep chunks of pavement from going through the windshields."

A fiasco was expected, and that's just what happened, with Junior right in the midst of it.

Speeding through the fourth turn early in the race, Junior hit a gaping hole in the pavement and blew a tire. He careened through a dirt area between the track and pit road and destroyed the structure that was to serve as Victory Lane. After repairs to the car, Junior returned to the track and eventually completed 287 of the race's 400 laps. Meanwhile, his friend Jack Smith was motoring to a five-lap lead with about 75 miles to go. Then a piece of sharp asphalt punctured Smith's fuel tank, and a lanky Tennesseean named Joe Lee Johnson, no relation to Junior, won the race. It was to be his only major victory.

Junior's perseverance in continuing to race after the tangle with the Victory Lane fence and stand apparently gave him a finish of thirtieth in a sixty-car field. However, he eventually was listed as finishing fifty-ninth. "NASCAR disqualified me, Richard Petty, Lee Petty, Bob Welborn, and a couple of other guys for cutting across that dirt area, which is now grass, to get to pit road," says Junior. "Best I remember, every one of us had flat tires. I know I did, and I wasn't goin' to try to drive all the way back around the track with a blowed-out tire. That would have torn the car all to pieces. Plus, a feller might have got caught in one of those gaping holes and been forced to stop, then been hit by another car.

"What surprised me so much about the whole thing is that NASCAR let us keep on racing that day and didn't say nothing about us being disqualified. That didn't come out 'til the race was over. They let us run, then wouldn't pay us."

Junior won twice more in 1960, taking races in late summer on the short tracks at Hickory and at South Boston, Virginia. His season statistics were thirty-four starts, the three victories, fourteen top fives, eighteen top tens, seventh place in the point standings, and earnings of $38,989.

In 1961, Junior took on a new team that produced rousing results. He found it back home in the hills of Wilkes County. "Fred and Rex Lovette, who had co-founded the Holly Farms poultry company at Wilkesboro with some

other businessmen, liked racin' a lot and they wanted to get into it as car owners," says Junior. "We were friends, so they asked me to drive for them and I agreed. We chose Pontiacs for our racecars."

The season got off to a scary start. Junior and Fireball Roberts were racing side by side for the lead late in a 100-mile preliminary to the Daytona 500 when Junior ran over a sharp piece of metal debris, cutting a tire. Junior's Pontiac and Richard Petty's Plymouth collided. Petty's car became airborne and flew over the first turn railing. While Richard was zooming out of the track, Junior simultaneously slammed head-on into the railing. Richard escaped injury except for some bits of glass in his eyes from a shattered windshield. Later that day, in a second qualifying race, Lee Petty, incredibly, went over the fourth turn rail and suffered injuries that ended his driving career.

"I tore down ten or eleven of the posts holding the rails," says Junior. "Then I spun down to the apron and across the grass to the inside fence.

"I thought everything had settled down, so I took my belts off and started crawlin' out of the car. Then, I saw a guy comin' off the first turn, spinning right toward me. I jumped back in the car for protection.

"He hit me so hard I pushed the steering wheel through the windshield. My chin hit the steering wheel right where the horn would be on a passenger car. Blood spewed everywhere. I thought my throat had been cut.

"Back in those days, Big Bill France sometimes cruised during races along a perimeter road that went around the racetrack just inside the inner guardrail. He came by just as I got out of the car with blood all over me.

"Bill was driving a white Buick Riviera convertible with white leather seats.

"I said, 'Take me to the hospital!'

"Bill's eyes were wide at the sight of me—I guess he was sort of shocked—and he said, 'You can't get in here! You'll get blood on my seats!'

"I said, 'I don't care about your damn seats. Take me to the hospital.'

"He got me to the infield infirmary, and on the way, I did get blood all over the inside of his car. It took several stitches to sew up the gash on my chin.

"Despite the wreck, which pushed my engine into the cockpit, I got in the 500 in another Pontiac. I started forty-third, but before the first pit stop for tires I was leading. It took me just thirty-three laps—all under the green flag—to pass everybody ahead of me. I really thought we were going to win the 500. But then a bunch of paper hotdog wrappers blew onto the grille and stuck there, and on the forty-fifth lap the engine overheated and failed."

Junior's stirring charge to start the Daytona 500 was a sign of dandy things to come for him and his new team, which included widely respected crew chief/mechanic Crawford Clements. Fred Johnson, Junior's brother, also was a member of the team. Junior drove the Lovette-fielded Pontiac to seven victories, all on short tracks.

At Martinsville (Virginia) Speedway on April 30, 1961, one of the most remarkable rallies in NASCAR history took place as Junior charged from four laps down to then-leader Fred Lorenzen to beat Emanuel Zervakis by four laps. Even after mounting his big lead, Junior maintained a characteristic full-bore pace. All the while Rex Lovette and the crew were imploring him to slow down.

"I had radio communication from the car to Rex that day," says Junior. "As far as I know, this was the first time anyone tried using radios during a race. Holly Farms had shortwave

Junior's car was severely damaged at Daytona soon after he collided with Petty. While his car sat idly near the inside fence, another car came spinning towards him, smashing the entire front of Junior's car. "He hit me so hard I pushed the steering wheel through the windshield," says Junior, who suffered a lacerated chin. (Daytona Racing Archives)

**"Well, Rex kept cussin' and raisin' the dickens on the radio." Junior beams at the recollection. "I grinned and gave Rex the thumbs-up," says Junior. "I don't think I ever saw a madder man."**

radios that were used in the business by truck drivers picking up chickens from farmers. Rex and Fred hit on the idea of using a couple of these radios to talk to me in the racecar while they watched from pit road or the infield.

"When I got so far ahead, the Lovettes and the pit guys decided I should back off a little bit, and, to a point, I did. To me, I had slowed down. But not enough for them. I felt the car was set up in such a way that I needed to run fairly fast to keep it working right. If I'd slowed down any more, the car wouldn't have done what it was supposed to. Well, Rex kept cussin' and raisin' the dickens on the radio. He was on there so much that he was distractin' me, so I cut the darn thing off.

"I started tappin' on the top of my helmet each time I came by our pit. That was the prearranged sign that I couldn't hear any radio messages." The crew responded by repeatedly displaying a pit board to Junior with the message "E-Z" chalked on it in big letters. He ignored the order. Rex Lovette became very angered and exasperated. During Junior's final scheduled pit stop Lovette fetched a sledgehammer from among the team's tools. He strode to the pit wall and waved the heavy hammer at Junior in a threatening fashion. Junior beams at the recollection. "I grinned and gave Rex the thumbs-up," says Junior. "I don't think I ever saw a madder man."

There was widespread anger later in the 1961 season on August 13 following Junior's victory in the Western North Carolina 500. Approximately 10,000 fans had gathered at the Asheville-Weaverville Speedway atop a ridge to watch both the race and a possible confrontation between Big Bill France and Curtis Turner, who was attempting to unionize the drivers. Turner was a no-show, but a controversy developed nonetheless.

Shortly after the 500-lap event began on the half-mile track, the asphalt pavement began breaking apart. Large chunks flew everywhere, including into the main grandstand. Several spectators were struck by chunks of asphalt. A young schoolteacher from nearby Yancey County, Louetta Randolph, was knocked unconscious when hit in the temple.

Track conditions deteriorated to the point that NASCAR alerted the teams that the race would end shortly after reaching halfway to make the event official. On lap 258, both the red and checkered flags were shown. Junior held the lead, three laps ahead of Joe Weatherly.

An estimated 4,000 fans were outraged by the premature conclusion and used a large truck to block the crossover road leading from the infield. The drivers and their teams were trapped inside the track. A riot ensued as unruly fans demanded refunds.

A would-be mediator among the fans was picked up by the protesters and hurled into a pond near the track. Lawmen called to the scene were too outnumbered to disperse the crowd. Finally, with darkness drawing near, the competitors lost patience.

"Pop Ergle, a giant of a guy who worked for Bud Moore's team, went to the gate at the crossover to tell the people blocking us that we were coming out," says Junior. "One of the ringleaders had a two-by-four board, and he poked Pop in the belly with it. That was a big mistake. Pop took the two-by-four away from the guy and started swinging it. Before long the place cleared out and we left."

Junior finished sixth in the 1961 point standings. In addition to the seven wins, he posted nine other top-five finishes and twenty-two top tens, and he won $28,540 in forty starts.

The asphalt track surface at Asheville broke apart during the 1961 Western North Carolina 500 and caused dangerous driving conditions. One piece of flying debris broke Junior's windshield. Despite the hazards, Junior led all 258 laps and took the checkered flag when the race was stopped for safety concerns. (Don Hunter)

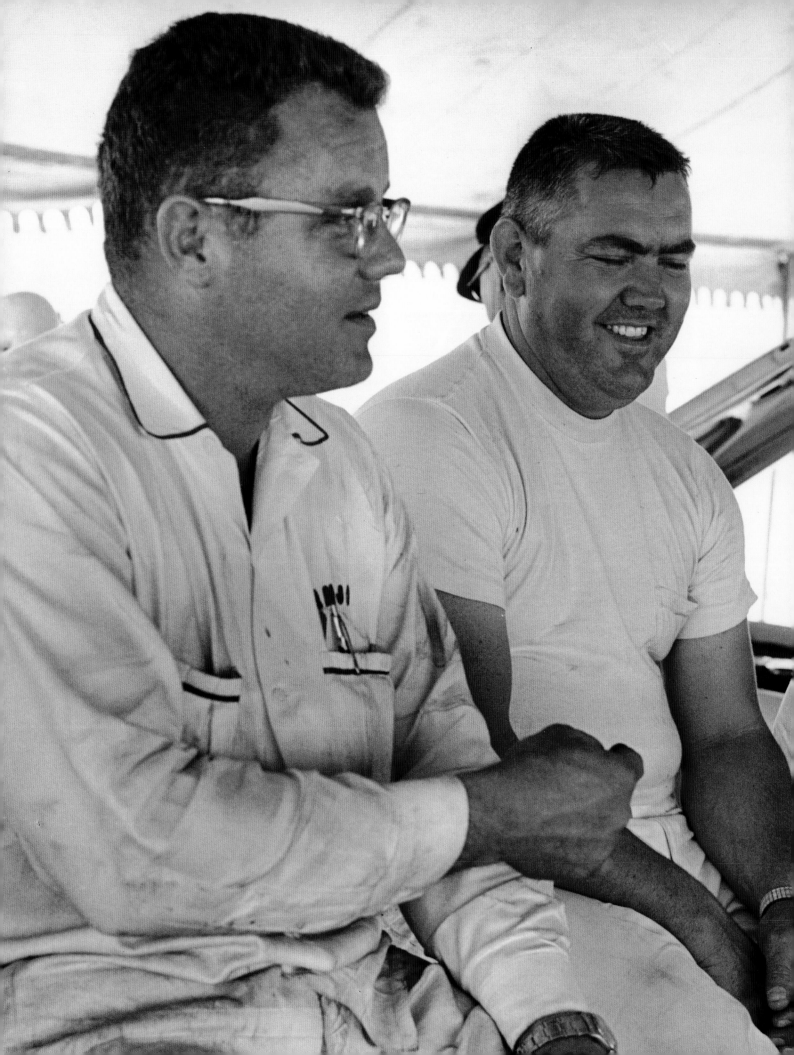

# CHAPTER SIX

The temperature was scorchingly hot on Labor Day in 1962 and the heat took a toll on both tires and drivers during the Southern 500. There were several hard crashes because of blown tires and as the 500 rolled on, several drivers were on the verge of heat exhaustion.

Among those who experienced tire problems was Junior, who hit the railing midway through the race. He spent two laps in his pit getting the fenders pulled back to prevent tire rub. Nevertheless, Junior was shown as the leader by NASCAR scoring over the last one-fifth of the race.

Junior was flagged the winner. Following in the top six, according to NASCAR, were Marvin Panch, David Pearson, Larry Frank, Jim Paschal, and Richard Petty.

Frank, running on a rim in a shower of sparks, braked his car to a stop and parked on the grass right across the track from the press box. He had blown a tire just after crossing the finish line.

Doubts about the scoring were expressed immediately by some members of the media, fans, and competitors. Lee Petty filed a protest on behalf of Richard. Representatives

## "It was a sickening sight."

Above right: Junior climbs from his car after being flagged the winner in the 1962 Southern 500 at Darlington Raceway. The scoring of the race was immediately protested, and at midnight NASCAR admitted a mistake had been made and awarded the victory to Larry Frank. It was Frank's first and only Grand National win. (Don Hunter)

Opposite: Junior drove the 1964 Ford owned by Banjo Matthews (left) at the World 600 at Charlotte Motor Speedway. During the race Fireball Roberts was tragically burned after his car careened into the inner wall and burst into flames. Roberts was avoiding a collision between Junior and Ned Jarrett. (Don Hunter)

57

During the 1963 season Junior increased the number of events he competed in, driving in 33 races and scoring seven victories. Six of the triumphs and all nine of his poles were in the Holly Farms car owned by Rex Lovette. (Southern MotoRacing)

of Frank also protested. Weary from the oppressive heat and hurting with blistered eyelids, Frank left the track for a nearby motel while NASCAR coped with the controversy.

In the post-race winner's interview Junior was asked what he planned to do with his winner's share of approximately $20,000. "I'm going to build some more chicken houses on my farm," answered Junior.

Around midnight NASCAR issued a revised finishing order among the top six. Frank was listed as the winner, followed by Junior, Panch, Pearson, Petty, and Paschal. It was explained that a scorer had shorted Frank a lap. Frank's margin of victory over Junior was placed at 5 seconds. It was to prove the only triumph at NASCAR's major level for Frank.

Bloys Britt, the late Associated Press motorsports writer based in Charlotte, wryly observed that "Junior counted his chicken houses before they got built."

"NASCAR went to great pains to show me where the mistake was made. And they had a fairly convincing case, I guess," Junior now concedes. "But what upset me was NASCAR not catching the error sooner. They'd showed me in first place for a long time. If I'd known I actually was running second to Larry, I think I could have caught and passed him pretty easily."

Despite the solid success of 1961, the Holly Farms/ Johnson team adopted new plans for the 1962 season, undertaking what was termed "a limited schedule."

Junior explains: "We decided to just pick certain races to run. We stuck pretty much to the area of the country where Holly Farms at that time was doing business."

Salvaging the 1962 season somewhat for Junior was a single victory. It was a major one, coming in the National 400 in October at Charlotte Motor Speedway. Junior, driving a Pontiac fielded by Ray Fox, dominated the race,

leading 204 of 267 laps. In finishing two laps ahead of runner-up Fireball Roberts, Junior averaged a sizzling 132.085 MPH, then a track record. "That was a real special win to me," says Junior. "The new Charlotte track was the closest superspeedway to home, Wilkes County, and I naturally wanted to win there. Plus, there were a lot of fans and friends in the area that got a lot of pleasure out of me doing well at Charlotte."

In twenty-three starts in 1962, Junior had six other top-five finishes, eight top tens, and $34,840 in winnings. He wound up twentieth in the point standings.

In the 1963 season, Junior was more active. He drove thirty races for the Lovette-owned team, two for Fox, and one for Bill Stroppe. Switching to Chevrolets, Junior scored seven victories—six in the Holly Farms cars and one with Fox.

The win with Fox came in a 100-mile qualifying event leading to the Daytona 500. Junior proved just how great a force the aerodynamic draft could be by averaging a then-amazing 164.083 MPH, faster than his pole-winning time-trial speed of 163.681. Junior looked strong for the 500, but a faulty distributor sidelined him just twenty-six laps into the race.

However, six more victories followed at regular intervals in a season marked by a sizzling rivalry between Junior and rising Ford star Fred Lorenzen.

Junior scored twice in March, winning at Hillsborough, North Carolina, and at Hickory. France co-promoted the show on the Hillsborough dirt track and brought in glamorous movie star Jayne Mansfield as a guest to attract a larger crowd. "At that time she was about as big a star as Marilyn Monroe, so a lot of people at the race that day went sort of wild," says Junior. "When Jayne came down to take part in the Victory Lane deal, she was about mobbed. Some fans were grabbing at her, and she was scared. I felt sorry for her.

Junior's victory on the Hillsborough dirt track included a purse of $1,550 and a kiss from movie star Jayne Mansfield. Junior held Mansfield's son so she and her husband, Mickey Hargitay (far right), could keep the surging crowd at bay. "At the time she was about as big a star as Marilyn Monroe," Junior recalls. (Southern MotoRacing)

After winning at Hickory in March 1963, Junior announced that car owner John Chalik had offered him a ride for the Indianapolis 500 in May. The car failed to reach the required average of 170 mph and never qualified for the race, so Junior returned home to Wilkes County to rejoin the NASCAR tour. (Bob Janelle)

Junior rests before the National 400 at
Charlotte Motor Speedway in 1963.
Junior's No. 3 Chevrolet is next to
pole-winner Marvin Panch's No. 21 Ford.
Earlier in the week Junior and car owner
Ray Fox had learned that Chevrolet was
pulling out of NASCAR. (Don Hunter)

Dominating the National 400, Junior led 209 of the race's 267 laps and easily beat rival Fred Lorenzen by 12 seconds. On the left in Victory Lane is Miss Firebird, Linda Vaughn. (Don Hunter)

She had a young son with her. I held the little boy in Victory Lane so she could defend herself."

After winning at Hickory later in the month, Junior revealed a deal in which he'd attempt to qualify for the Indianapolis 500. "A real nice guy from Daytona Beach that I'd got to know, John Chalik, had some open-cockpit Champ cars and he asked me to drive for him," says Junior. "I'd listened to the Indy 500 on the radio for years and always wondered what it'd be like to be in that race."

Junior and Bobby Unser became Indy rookies as team-mates in Chalik's cars. However, the cars weren't very fast and both drivers were unable to average the required 170 MPH laps.

"I was hopeful after I had the crew put a stock car racing setup on my car and we immediately went seven or eight miles an hour faster than before," Junior says. "But even this didn't get us up to the speed we needed. So I came on back home and Bobby Unser went with another team and got in the 500. From the brief experience I had at Indianapolis, I've always felt I could have run there and been successful if I had decided to devote my time to that instead of NASCAR."

Back in his NASCAR ride, Junior won the pole for the World 600 at Charlotte. Lorenzen qualified second to set up a classic Chevy-Ford confrontation. Fans weren't disappointed as the two battled for the lead. Junior was in front the most, leading 262 of the 400 laps on the 1.5-mile track. He had led a stretch of 77 laps and was slightly ahead of his Ford foe with just 6 miles to go. Then the right rear tire blew on Junior's Chevy after being cut, and he had to pit for new rubber. "Somebody threw a beer bottle out of the grandstands right in front of me," recalls Junior. "I saw it come over the fence and break on the track, and I was going so fast I couldn't do a thing to avoid running through the pieces of glass."

Junior emerged from the pit still on the same lap but finished second, 35 seconds behind Lorenzen. Lorenzen's car ran out of gas en route to Victory Lane. Lorenzen said he likely would have overtaken Junior even had he not had the cut tire. Junior scoffs at the notion. "He hadn't run me down the whole race in that situation, and he certainly wasn't going to do it at the end," he says.

Junior enjoyed a measure of revenge later in June by beating Lorenzen in the Dixie 400 at Atlanta. He led the last thirty-three laps and won by 3 seconds. Junior won in August at Winston-Salem and in September at Hickory. Junior's incredibly cool nature showed at Hickory when he once more flipped his car in practice, then shook off the accident to win the race. When the NASCAR tour returned to Charlotte for the National 400, Junior got an extra measure of revenge. He trounced Lorenzen and everyone else in the field, leading a whopping 209 of the 267 laps. Junior simply motored away in the final 32 laps and finished 12 seconds in front of Lorenzen, the runner-up. Said Junior at the time, "Maybe now Freddie will quit bragging about outrunning me."

Junior's statistics for the 1963 season were thirty-three starts, the seven wins, thirteen top fives, fourteen top tens, and $67,350 in purses. He placed twelfth in the point standings.

**Far Left:** The No. 27 Ford looked decrepit following Junior's spectacular crash with Bud Moore in the wreck-filled 1964 Southern 500 at Darlington. When Junior spun out on lap 149, Moore slammed into him with so much force that the rear bumper was pushed to where the back seat would have been. (Daytona Racing Archives)

**Left:** During the October race at North Wilkesboro, Junior became nominally involved in the 1964 presidential race between Lyndon Johnson and Barry Goldwater. By printing these visors, speedway publicist Hank Schoolfield, a staunch Republican, took a humorous shot at President Johnson, the Democratic candidate, and his "birds"—wife Lady Bird and daughters Lynda Bird and Lucy Bird. Junior finished thirteenth in the race because of engine failure. (Southern MotoRacing)

Some of the darkest times in NASCAR history loomed on the horizon as the calendar turned to 1964. Popular driving champion Joe Weatherly, Jimmy Pardue, a Wilkes County neighbor of Junior's, and the famed Fireball Roberts all lost their lives in racing accidents. Weatherly was fatally injured during January's Motor Trend 500 on the Riverside road course in California. Pardue died of injuries he sustained at Charlotte in September while running a tire test for the track's 400-miler the next month.

On May 24, Roberts was caught in a bunched-up field on the eighth lap of the World 600 in Charlotte, with Junior and Ned Jarrett. The cars of Junior and Jarrett made contact between the first and second turns. Roberts took evasive action and spun off the second corner. Roberts's car slammed backward into an opening in the inner wall, ruptured the gas tank, and ignited the fuel. Jarrett's car spun to a stop nearby and quickly was engulfed in the flames. Junior's car carried on down the backstretch a ways. Jarrett exited his car quickly and was able to aid Roberts, who was suffering horrid burns, in getting free of the inferno in his cockpit.

Junior, visibly shaken, initially blamed himself for the accident after emerging from the infield infirmary. "I guess it's my fault," he said. "I lost control coming off the second turn." However, Jarrett exonerated Junior: "Junior hit a bump, then hit me. There was a lot of turbulence at the speed we were going, and it was easy to lose control."

"I remember that when I stopped spinning, the front end of my car was pinned against the wall," says Junior. "I got out and headed toward where Ned and Fireball had stopped. Ned was already out of his car and helping Fireball. It was about as big a fire as I've ever seen. And it was awful hot. So hot you couldn't hardly stand it. After Fireball was out of the car and leaned up against the wall, I saw how terrible his burns were. It was a sickening sight."

Roberts was taken to Memorial Hospital in Charlotte. At one point it appeared he would survive. But blood poisoning and pneumonia developed. He went into a coma and died on July 2.

"It's amazing to me that he lived very long at all, much less a month," Junior says. "It shows the strong spirit and fight he had in him."

Roberts's death shook the sport and led NASCAR to develop the self-sealing rubber fuel cell to replace metal gas tanks. In losing his life, Roberts was indirectly responsible for saving the lives of many other drivers.

During the fall of 1964 *Esquire* magazine ran an article written by Tom Wolfe. The piece was titled "Junior Johnson Is The Last American Hero—Yes!" Readers nationwide were fascinated, and not surprisingly, because of passages like this: "Junior was famous for the 'bootlegger turn,' or 'about-face,' in which, if the Alcohol Tax Agents had a roadblock up…he threw the car into second gear, cocked the wheel, stepped on the accelerator, and made the car's rear end skid around in a 180-degree arc…and tore back up the road exactly the way he had come from. God! The tax agents used to burn over Junior Johnson."

"That Wolfe guy was something else," Junior says with a chuckle. "He showed up down here in Wilkes County talkin' funny, with a New York accent, and wearin' fancy clothes, including spats. Spats! I doubt anybody in Wilkes County ever had seen spats, at least not in recent times. I didn't have much time to spend with him. I didn't figure he'd get much of a story. But somehow he got local people to talk to him and his story turned out pretty doggone good and accurate."

The *Esquire* article inspired a movie a few years later about Junior called *The Last American Hero.*

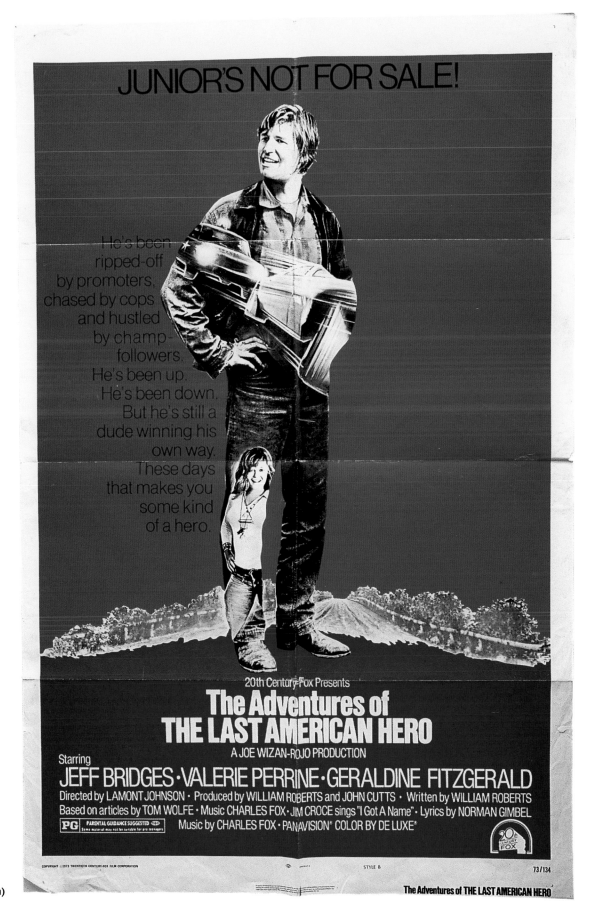

JUNIOR'S NOT FOR SALE!

He's been
ripped-off
by promoters,
chased by cops
and hustled
by champ-
followers.
He's been up.
He's been down.
But he's still a
dude winning his
own way.
These days
that makes you
some kind
of a hero.

20th Century-Fox Presents

**The Adventures of
THE LAST AMERICAN HERO**

A JOE WIZAN-ROJO PRODUCTION

Starring
**JEFF BRIDGES · VALERIE PERRINE · GERALDINE FITZGERALD**

Directed by LAMONT JOHNSON · Produced by WILLIAM ROBERTS and JOHN CUTTS · Written by WILLIAM ROBERTS
Based on articles by TOM WOLFE · Music CHARLES FOX · JIM CROCE sings "I Got A Name" · Lyrics by NORMAN GIMBEL

**PG** PARENTAL GUIDANCE SUGGESTED ⬛
Some material may not be suitable for pre-teenagers    Music by CHARLES FOX · PANAVISION® COLOR BY DE LUXE®

COPYRIGHT ©1973 TWENTIETH CENTURY-FOX FILM CORPORATION                          STYLE B                          73/134

The Adventures of THE LAST AMERICAN HERO

Inspired by Tom Wolfe's *Esquire* magazine article on Junior, *The Last American Hero* was released in June of 1973 and starred Jeff Bridges as a young moonshiner and racer, "Junior Jackson." At the Charlotte premiere Junior gave his approval saying, "It was pretty much the way it was." (Wm. Craig Brabson)

# CHAPTER SEVEN

Junior made seventeen of his starts in 1964 at the wheel of Fords fielded by Banjo Matthews, who was destined to become a leading car-builder, with Junior among his top customers. Two of Junior's victories came in Matthews' machines.

Junior decided to stick with Ford when he fielded his own cars in 1965. The result was one of the greatest performances in NASCAR history. Junior "batted" .361, winning thirteen times in thirty-six starts.

The 1965 season was something of a sentimental journey for Junior. He was increasingly thinking about ending his driving days. It was appropriate that some of Junior's triumphs came at tracks where NASCAR roots reached deep.

He won another Daytona 500 qualifying race, this time passing Lorenzen on the last lap for the victory. He won on a dirt track, breaking a ten-year drought at the Richmond Fairgrounds in March. He led 356 of 400 laps in April to score at home, North Wilkesboro Speedway, for the first time since October of 1958. He edged Dick Hutcherson at Bristol in May to become the first driver to win on tubeless tires. The Bristol triumph started a

## "Junior was pure driver."

Above right: This promotional postcard for Junior's sponsor, Holly Farms, shows one of the three Fords Junior used in 1965. The team shop and garage in the background was located at the Holly Farms Poultry plant in Wilkesboro. (Southern MotoRacing)

Opposite: Waiting for the start of the 1964 Wilkes 400 at North Wilkesboro, Junior and Matthews (right) qualified on the pole with Matthew's 1964 Ford. The engine failed on lap 297 of the 400-lap race, leaving the team with a thirteenth place finish. Junior made seventeen starts during the season for Matthews, but decided in 1965 to field his own Ford cars. (Southern MotoRacing)

sensational tear by Junior, during which he won four of the next five races.

Six days after winning at Bristol, Junior dominated at Darlington, leading 197 of 219 laps in the Rebel 300 and finishing 3 seconds ahead of Darel Dieringer. Bud Moore, Dieringer's car owner, protested the win shortly after the checkered flag. Moore contended that Junior had slid through his pit stall during a stop, which violated the rules. The outcome was debated at NASCAR headquarters in Daytona Beach for two days. Finally, officials ruled in Junior's favor because the pit stall he had slid into was vacant—no team was using it.

Memories of the 1962 Southern 500 fiasco, when a scoring error took away his finish, haunted Junior during NASCAR's deliberations. "I really wanted that win because I knew I'd only race again at Darlington another time or two," says Junior. "To me, that track was the biggest challenge in NASCAR, so I got more enjoyment out of racin' there than anywhere. Because the two ends of the speedway are so different—the track is shaped like an egg, with the west end sort of pointed—it requires compromising in the chassis setup. This is a difficult deal to achieve, and I liked figuring that out.

"You had to drive your car right against the railing to get through the fourth turn [now the second turn]. This would scrape the paint off the right side of the car. This is how the term, 'The Darlington Stripe,' originated. Naturally, after you scraped along that railing enough times, the sheet metal got bent in on the right side tires. To avoid this, we started mounting springs horizontally on the right side of our car inside the sheet metal. As a result the sheet metal had some give to it. Once you got away from the wall, the springs would push the sheet metal back out and off the tires. You had to try all kind of tricks to run Darlington. It was my favorite track. Still is."

The weekend after his Rebel 300 victory, Junior triumphed twice. He beat old rival Ned Jarrett on May 15 at Winston-Salem's Bowman Gray Stadium, a football arena, then topped Jarrett again the next day at Hickory. "Ned had tough luck at Hickory, or I wouldn't have got him," concedes Junior. "He blew a tire with just two laps to go while leading and still managed to finish second."

Junior was winless in June. But he won twice in a twenty-four-hour period on July 8 and 9, scoring at Manassas, Virginia, and Old Bridge, New Jersey. At the Manassas track, not far from the Civil War battlefield, he led all but the first 4 laps of a 400-lap race. From Old Bridge, NASCAR's so-called "Northern Swing" rolled on to Islip, New York, for a 250-lap race on a tiny track measuring just two-tenths of a mile. Junior qualified fifth and on the 112th lap he moved into position to challenge pole winner Marvin Panch for the lead. Junior was making his move to pass going into the third turn when a problem developed.

"The darn throttle hung," recalls Junior, eyes sparkling. "It had done the same thing in practice, and I'd been able to turn the switch off and keep control of the car. We thought we had it fixed, but it happened again just when

Junior went on a midseason tear, winning four out of five races in May. After going winless in June, he and Nab (middle) regained their form and took back-to-back victories in Manassas, Virginia, and Old Bridge, New Jersey, on July 8 and 9. (Southern MotoRacing)

Since the beginning of his career, one of Junior's biggest rivals was Fred Lorenzen, shown here with Junior before the World 600 at Charlotte Motor Speedway. Two weeks earlier at North Wilkesboro, Junior and Lorenzen had rubbed cars en route to Junior's victory. After the race Junior said, "Me and Freddie fightin' it out was just like the old days." (Don Hunter)

While Junior received a kiss from the Bowman-Gray Stadium trophy girl for his victory in the 50-mile event, Nab was hit with a $100 fine by NASCAR. Controversy was sparked when Nab was asked to take the car to the inspection area by NASCAR official Dick Beaty. Nab followed the instructions, but one of Johnson's mechanics removed the car before an inspection could take place. No protest was filed, but Nab was fined for the suspicious action. (Southern MotoRacing)

Despite his car's reliability during the majority of the season, engine failures greatly hampered the team in the last three races. Junior led the first 45 laps of the American 500 in Rockingham before engine problems knocked him out of contention. He finished thirty-second. (Pal Parker)

Junior slips high into the wall at Martinsville Speedway during the Virginia 500 in April as young fans watch from the brush. Junior redeemed his crash later in the year by winning the Old Dominion 500 at Martinsville in September. (Southern MotoRacing)

The 1965 Ford team included (left to right, front row) Fred Lorenzen, Ned Jarrett, A.J. Foyt, (left to right, back row) Marvin Panch, Curtis Turner, Dick Hutcherson, Junior, and Cale Yarborough. At the end of the season Ford announced it was pulling out of the sport, which prompted Junior to consider retirement. (Don Hunter)

Right: Junior clowns with fellow Ford driver Tom Pistone. Junior had much to be happy about in 1965, posting one of his best seasons with thirteen victories and $62,215 in earnings. (Southern MotoRacing)

Far right: Junior gives Bobby Isaac a push during practice at North Carolina Motor Speedway. Isaac debuted in the 1965 season finale at Moyock, North Carolina, and was the first driver to run for Junior after his retirement. (Dozier Mobley)

me and Marvin were having a devil of a race. I tried to back off, but I couldn't. I went through the fence, bounced pretty high, and hit a utility pole. The impact with the pole busted the fuel pump and the car caught fire immediately. I landed on my wheels, so I was able to get out pretty quick. My car came to rest in the parking lot next to a little ol' concession stand. I hit the stand just enough to jar it. The blaze was so big it looked like the stand might catch fire, too.

"Well, a woman was operating the stand, and the accident really scared her, which is understandable. I helped her get out of the stand and back away from the fire. At this time I noticed she was about seven months pregnant. She was so excited I don't know why she didn't have that baby right there."

Following Junior's incident with the concession stand were more victories. He led all but the first of 250 laps to win at Winston-Salem in August. And all but 19 of 500 laps to triumph at Martinsville in September. Richard Petty was the runner-up in both races. On October 3, to the roaring approval of a huge, standing-room-only crowd, Junior won at North Wilkesboro, beating a promising young newcomer named Cale Yarborough by two laps. Earlier, Lorenzen had shaken a puzzling slump to challenge strongly before falling victim to engine failure. "Me and Freddie fightin' it out was just like the old days," says Junior. "It was a lot of fun."

That enjoyment would have to last Junior a long, long time. Although a few more starts remained, the autumn of his driving career was at hand. That golden fall afternoon at the track in the Brushy Mountains was the final time that Junior would go to Victory Lane as the winning driver.

Like in a storybook, the last of his fifty NASCAR victories had come on the track where he'd first raced as a teenager after he had taken the mule to the barn and fetched his shoes.

Junior ran the next three races following his North Wilkesboro victory, but mechanical problems sidelined him prematurely in each. Nevertheless, Junior finished with sensational statistics: the thirteen victories, five additional top-five finishes, nineteen top tens, twelfth place in the point standings, and $62,215 in earnings, good for third place on the money list.

For the 1965 season finale, the fifty-fifth race of the season, Junior hired fellow Tar Heel Bobby Isaac to drive the No. 26 Ford at Moyock, North Carolina, in the Tidewater 250. Things went extremely well at the one-third-mile dog-racing track. Isaac won the pole and battled for the lead throughout before finishing second to Ned Jarrett, the circuit's champion. The Johnson/Isaac pairing then was forged for 1966. "Ford was pulling out of the sport, pulling the factory support, so it seemed like a good time for me to retire as a driver," says Junior. "The situation with the manufacturers being in and out and then in and out again was gettin' aggravating."

It seemed a good match. Isaac, like Junior, hailed from a rural area, little Catawba, North Carolina, only 40 miles from Wilkes County. And, like Junior, Isaac was immensely aggressive. Isaac had started his driving career at Hickory Speedway in jalopy races. There was a humorous local contention at that time: "When Bobby Isaac runs, one of two things is going to happen—he's either going to win the race or the fight afterward."

Johnson and Isaac shared a lot of the same tastes, including the movies. In the winter of 1965–66 the world premiere of a film about racing, *Red Line 7000*, was held in Charlotte. One of the characters was loosely based on Junior. Dozens of NASCAR figures were enticed to attend

the premiere, including the top drivers and team owners. The movie proved to be terrible. It was so bad that drivers Tom Pistone and Tiny Lund began making loud wisecracks about the ludicrous dialogue, amusing the audience.

Less than twenty minutes into the picture Junior and Bobby Isaac walked out in disgust. Their pairing, which had appeared so promising, lasted only a bit longer than their stay in that Charlotte theater. Isaac would drive but eight races for Junior, posting a best finish of second in the season opener at Augusta, Georgia. "Ford pulled out in a fuss with NASCAR, one of many boycotts in that era," says Junior, explaining the split. "They wanted all their cars and other stuff back from our shop, and I got it to them. Bobby wasn't going to sit out, and I don't blame him. He went looking for another ride."

Isaac's career later produced 37 victories overall and the championship in 1970. He died of complications from heat exhaustion suffered during a weekly race at Hickory in 1977.

Junior, despite his deep desire to retire, returned to the cockpit for eight starts in 1966, logging a top finish of fifth. Appropriately, Junior's last start came at the site of his very first one, North Wilkesboro Speedway. It happened on October 2 in the Wilkes 400.

Junior delighted adoring fans by winning the pole, the forty-seventh of his career, and leading the first seventy-six laps. He regained the lead on lap 112 and was going strong in first place when his engine failed during the 129th lap, forcing him from the race. Thus Junior Johnson held the same position on the final lap he completed that he'd held so often and so spectacularly in a driving career spanning fourteen seasons. He was in front.

Junior pulled behind the pit road wall at North Wilkesboro and crawled from the cockpit of a race car for the last time. "I didn't feel sad," recalls Junior. "I had held a notion for some time that I'd accomplished practically everything I'd set out to accomplish. I didn't have anything to prove to anybody, including myself. On top of this, driving wasn't fun anymore. The thrill was gone, even the excitement of the speed had gradually worn off. Like I said, I'd run faster in a liquor car than I ever did on racetracks, including Daytona, Charlotte, and Atlanta. I was quitting, and this time I stuck to it." Junior went into retirement with 50 victories in 313 starts, 69 other top-five finishes, 10 other top tens, and $275,910 in winnings.

While many others have compiled gaudier statistics, *Sports Illustrated* magazine published a special edition for NASCAR's 50th anniversary in 1998, naming Junior Johnson the sport's number-one driver of all time. Rated second through twelfth in a "Dandy Dozen" were David Pearson, Richard Petty, Bobby Allison, Dale Earnhardt, Darrell Waltrip, Cale Yarborough, Jeff Gordon, Herb Thomas, Fireball Roberts, Tim Flock, and Lee Petty.

*Sports Illustrated* made a compelling case for choosing Junior, citing his charging style and success in equipment that wasn't conducive to being run hard. Praised Richard Petty, the winner of 200 races and seven championships, "Most of us depended on other things to win, like strategy and the setup of our cars. Junior was pure driver." Though Junior was through driving race cars when he parked that Sunday afternoon in October of '66 at North Wilkesboro, by no means was he through winning.

Junior feeds his 2,700-pound prize bull on his farm in 1966. "I had held a notion for some time that I'd accomplished practically everything I'd set out to accomplish. I didn't have anything to prove to anybody, including myself," says Junior about his retirement. (NASCAR Winston Cup Scene Archives)

# CHAPTER EIGHT

Despite the temporary problem created by Ford's pullout in 1966, Junior enjoyed the role of team owner, fielding cars for someone else to drive.

After the departure of Isaac, Junior put four different men other than himself in the cockpits of his cars that season.

They were Indy Car driver Gordon Johncock, Darel Dieringer, A.J. Foyt, and two of Junior's old rivals, Curtis Turner and Fred Lorenzen.

A few days before a race at Columbia Speedway in South Carolina, word was sent to Turner by NASCAR officials that he'd be required to wear a suit in order to compete.

Turner showed up at the track wearing handsome, well-tailored business attire.

NASCAR had meant, of course, a driving suit.

"You didn't specify what kind of suit," Turner dead-panned to the officials.

Turner's presence in a car prepared by Junior Johnson had been heavily promoted to attract a big crowd, so denying the driver entry into the race was out of the question.

"Curtis stuck to his guns—er, suit. I remember he still was wearing a tie when he put his helmet on," says Junior.

## "We ain't buddies no more."

Above right: In 1966, in his first Daytona 500 as strictly an owner, Junior entered Fords for Bobby Isaac, who came in twenty-first, and A.J. Foyt, who was thirty-third. Richard Petty won the race and became the first two-time winner of the Daytona 500. (Don Hunter)

Opposite: Curtis Turner (26) and Cale Yarborough (21) jockey for position in the Southern 500 at Darlington Raceway. Yarborough finished eleventh and Turner wrecked on lap 348, finishing four-teenth. It was one of three races Turner drove for Junior. (Dozier Mobley)

On the driver carousel for Junior in 1966 was Gordon Johncock, who ran two races in the No. 26 Ford at the end of the season. Johncock's best finish was fourth in the National 500 at Charlotte Motor Speedway. Here he battles with Jack Bowsher (No. 33) for position in the race. (Pal Parker)

Responding to a request from John Holman of the famous Holman-Moody operation, Junior fielded a Ford for Lorenzen in the Dixie 400 at Atlanta in August. Junior had an informal working agreement with Holman, a close friend. Junior and his crew arrived at the raceway with a car that immediately ignited a barrage of fireworks and howls of protest among rivals. The car was supposed to be a Ford, but its profile looked like nothing that had come out of Detroit. The front sloped downward, the roof was cut very low, and the rear end was raised. Because the car carried Holly Farms' yellow paint scheme, it quickly was nicknamed "The Banana." Other names were less kind. Like "Junior's Joke."

Wily Smokey Yunick, the imaginative engineer/team owner, had brought an equally strange-looking Chevelle to Atlanta. A ruckus raged over both cars, but each was cleared to race by NASCAR, which rejected three other machines. Turner won the pole in Yunick's Chevy while Lorenzen qualified third. Both were to lead in their "modifieds," but just past halfway a distributor failure sidelined Turner and a blown tire led to a crash that forced Lorenzen to park.

"I built that car because Holman was a friend and asked me to help him out," says Junior with a smile. "He said, 'Build something that will run,' and I did. We had a heck of a time getting through inspection. We took that car to body shops all around Atlanta making changes here and there before we got it close enough for NASCAR to approve." It was the first—and only—time the car with the body that resembled a banana was allowed to race. NASCAR, sensitive to a barrage of criticism, quietly told Junior not to bring it back.

Seeking more driver stability, Junior settled on Dieringer for 1967. The pairing produced plenty of promise as the season began. Dieringer finished second in a qualifying race for the Daytona 500 and was sixth in the big show. A second and a third followed in the Fireball 300 and Southeastern 500 at Asheville-Weaverville, North Carolina, and Bristol, Tennessee, respectively.

On April 16, Dieringer, starting from the pole, led all 400 laps at North Wilkesboro and won the Gwyn Staley Memorial race by a lap. It was a euphoric experience for the whole team, but especially Dieringer. "This is Junior's home country," he said. "It means so much to me to have a part in a win like this for him." It was to prove the only victory that Dieringer would achieve in a Johnson car.

"We started having bad luck after that, and it continued on through the summer," says Junior. "Darel crashed at

Junior's 1966 Ford was nicknamed "The Banana" for its yellow paint scheme, downward sloped front end, raised rear end, and low-cut roof. As a favor to John Holman from the Holman-Moody team, Junior prepared "The Banana" for Fred Lorenzen in the Dixie 400 at Atlanta in August. Lorenzen led 23 laps before crashing 119 laps from the finish. (Don Hunter)

"The Banana" shows off its oddly curved backside, and how different it looked compared to its competitors. Curtis Turner's 1966 Chevrolet sits in front of it and has a standard downward slope to its rear end. On the right, Earl Balmer's 1965 Dodge shows the difference between a conventional roof line and window area, and the low-cut roof with narrowed window areas on "Junior's Joke." (Daytona Racing Archives)

Left: Junior settled on Lee Roy Yarbrough to replace Dieringer before the end of the season, saying "his style was pure aggressiveness. He had this fearlessness about him." Yarbrough debuted with Junior in the Wilkes 400 at North Wilkesboro and finished third. (Don Hunter)

Opposite: Junior gives NASCAR official John Bruner an earful after Yarbrough was black-flagged while in the lead just 33 laps from the finish in the 1967 Atlanta 500. Yarbrough was penalized for jumping a green flag, and then ignoring the consultation flag for five laps. Cale Yarborough won the race, Yarbrough finished second. (NASCAR Winston Cup Scene Archives)

Martinsville in September, and the guy running Ford's show in NASCAR at the time, Charlie Gray, wanted me to make a change. So we let Darel go."

Hired to join Junior's team was a young firebrand from Florida, LeeRoy Yarbrough. No relation to Cale Yarborough (note the different spellings of the last name), Yarbrough had gained a lot of attention in driving hot, powerful modified cars around the southeast. He showed his great potential for the NASCAR big time by winning the 1966 National 400 at Charlotte in a Dodge. "There were a lot of good young drivers coming along around 1967 and '68," says Junior. "To me, LeeRoy was ahead of the rest of them because his style was pure aggressiveness. He had this fearlessness about him. I saw that absolutely was going to be needed because the cars were starting to run so much faster than ever before on the big tracks. You had to have somebody with strong nerve to drive them."

Yarbrough posted a best finish of third in three starts for Junior late in 1967. In 1968 success came quickly, beginning with the Daytona 500. Yarbrough ran strongly in the front pack and was the leader during laps 177 through 196 of the 200-lap race. Then Yarbrough swept ahead and won by a second. Twice more in the season's first half Yarbrough finished as the runner-up in superspeedway races to the rival with the similar surname.

Then on July 14, in a 300-miler at Trenton, New Jersey, LeeRoy broke through to Victory Lane after starting on the pole and leading all but fifteen laps. Three weeks later the team scored again, taking the Dixie 500 at Atlanta. "We didn't win again in '68, but we wound up having a pretty good season for a first-year team," recalls Junior, whose outfit had ten other top-five finishes and winnings of $85,479 in only twenty starts. "We saw enough to know that we could figure on a great year in '69."

"Great" doesn't adequately describe what the Johnson team accomplished in 1969. The combination of Junior's cars and leadership and LeeRoy's driving ability produced one of the most storied seasons in NASCAR history. Yarbrough played the aerodynamic draft discovered by Johnson nine years earlier perfectly in the Daytona 500, pulling a slingshot pass of Charlie Glotzbach in the third turn on the last lap to dramatically win the race. "I'm going crazy; the crew is going crazy!" Yarbrough exulted in Victory Lane.

Cool calculation in the team's pit led to the opportunity to go crazy. Junior and crew chief Herb Nab figured Yarbrough's pit stops into a sequence that would allow them to put on tires of a softer compound for the decisive dash to the checkered flag. During that era NASCAR had no rules like those of today that strictly limit what type of tires may be used. So Junior ordered supersoft tires, nicknamed "gumballs," put on the right side of the Yarbrough-driven Ford during the final pit stop with twenty laps to go. The tires were short on durability but long on speed, producing great adhesion in the turns, thus faster lap times.

When Glotzbach's team, owned and led by Cotton Owens, opted for tires of a regular, harder compound, Chargin' Charlie was a sitting duck, never mind that he emerged from pit road with an 11-second lead on Yarbrough. "Me and Cotton were staying at the same motel in Daytona Beach, right across the highway from the racetrack," remembers Junior. "After the 500 I went over there to clean up before heading home. I ran into Cotton and he looked at me real hurt-like and said, 'We ain't buddies no more.' I said, 'Hell, Cotton, I didn't pass your car. LeeRoy did.' Cotton laughed and said, 'That he did.'"

Like Cotton Owens, a lot of rivals would suffer at the hands of the LeeRoy Yarbrough–Junior Johnson

On July 4 Yarbrough stormed to victory in the Firecracker 400, giving him a 1969 season sweep of Daytona. Nab moved the exhaust pipes from the side of the car to below the rear bumper the night before the race, making it difficult for cars to draft Yarbrough. The hot exhaust fumes either overheated the trailing car or caused the driver to get nauseous from the smell. (Don Hunter)

combination in 1969. Victory No. 2 came in a wreck-marred Rebel 400 at Darlington. No. 3 followed in the World 600 at Charlotte, in which Yarbrough led 264 of 400 laps, including the final 239. The victory margin was a whopping two laps as the team captured the second jewel in the sport's Triple Crown. LeeRoy and Junior made it a season sweep at Daytona by taking the Firecracker 400 on July 4. This was followed by an August triumph in Atlanta's Dixie 500.

These wins intensely fueled speculation about the Johnson outfit's chance of winning the Southern 500 on Labor Day at Darlington to become the first Triple Crown team in history. "We sort of downplayed the talk, but we really wanted to do it," Junior now concedes. Expectations—and pressure—grew when LeeRoy qualified fourth.

The sky was dark and ominous on race day, September 1, 1969. The action matched the setting as engine after engine failed and hard crashes developed. A violent thunderstorm forced a lengthy red flag period.

Finally, the rain stopped and the race resumed. It was obvious darkness would fall before 500 miles could be completed. NASCAR officials decided to flag the event to a conclusion after 230 laps, or 316 miles. All the front-runners pitted for fresh tires on lap 200. David Pearson and his Holman-Moody team opted for gumballs, as the Johnson team had in the Daytona 500. This time, Junior decided on a reverse strategy, going for tires of a harder compound.

"I just had a hunch," Junior recalls. "I figured that tires wore a bit more at Darlington than Daytona, so the harder compound might be the better choice." Indeed, as the race neared an end, Pearson began losing traction in the turns. The onrushing Yarbrough had just enough time to overtake the leader, diving low in the third turn on the final lap to surge ahead and take a courageous win.

They had achieved the first Daytona 500, Charlotte 600, Southern 500 sweep. The magnitude of the accomplishment can be measured by this fact: Through 1998 only two other drivers won those three races in the same season—David Pearson in 1975 and Jeff Gordon in 1997.

"I'm very proud of winning those three races even today," says Junior. "There were some very strong teams at that time: the Wood Brothers and Cale, David Pearson and Holman-Moody, Buddy Baker and Cotton Owens, Bobby Allison and Mario Rossi, Donnie Allison and Banjo, Richard Petty's team, Charlie Glotzbach and Ray Nichels. It took a lot of effort to beat 'em any time, much less in the biggest races."

Just two weeks after the Johnson-Yarbrough combination made such positive news for NASCAR at Darlington, the sport was in controversy at Talladega, Alabama. For months Big Bill France had hyped the grand opening of his new track, Alabama International Motor Speedway, at 2.66 miles both bigger and faster than its sister speedway in Daytona Beach. Similar to the opening of Charlotte Motor Speedway nine years earlier, there was trouble. The speed of the cars had outrun tire technology at that time. As drivers came within a tick of topping 200 MPH, their tires were wearing dangerously, and some even shredded.

The competitors had recently organized with the goal of gaining a say in how the sport was run, forming what they called the Professional Drivers Association. France called it a union and steadfastly said he wouldn't recognize it. So a strong undercurrent of suspicion and tension aggravated the tire wear situation. The drivers asked France to postpone the inaugural Talladega 500 until tire engineers from Firestone and Goodyear could develop a compound strong enough to withstand the soaring speeds at the new superspeedway. France refused.

On Saturday, September 13, the star drivers, including Yarbrough, discussed a walkout, or boycott. France

**Above:** At Darlington, Junior made the call for harder compound tires on Yarbrough's last pit stop, giving the driver enough traction to whip past David Pearson on the last lap and win the Southern 500. With the victory, Yarbrough became the first driver to win NASCAR's Triple Crown—the Daytona 500, Charlotte 600, and Southern 500. On the right of Yarbrough is his wife, Gloria, and Nab. (Pal Parker)

**Left:** Nab, crew member Turkey Minton, Junior, and Yarbrough brand their car with a dollar sign after winning the Dixie 500 and $18,620 in prize money. Standing behind them is crew member Francis Allen. Yarbrough had been suffering from the flu the week before the race and had to take a flu shot that morning to compete. (Dozier Mobley)

Yarbrough worked hard for Junior in 1969, posting seven wins and $193,611 in earnings. The achievements earned Yarbrough Ford's Driver of the Year award. (Pal Parker)

accosted them in the garage area and there were angry exchanges. To Yarbrough, France said, "LeeRoy, you're an airplane pilot. Consider this tire problem like you would a storm when you're in your plane. Slow down to work your way around it." To which Yarbrough replied, "Bill, when the storm is as bad as what we've got at this track, I don't even take off."

Simultaneously, Junior and other team owners were meeting in another corner of the garage area. "We were trying to figure out who we could put in our cars in case our regular drivers went through with their threat to walk out," says Junior. "Best I remember, me, Banjo Matthews, Glen Wood, John Holman, and Ralph Moody, all the Ford guys, were huddling to decide what we could do.

A lot of expense was involved. Plus, the team owners wanted to accommodate France and his new track, as well as themselves.

"Then Big Bill drove up, madder than hell," continues Junior. "He barked out, 'You've got fifteen minutes to get your cars on the track!' Well, that turned a lot of us off. We didn't appreciate it, getting an ultimatum like that when we were trying to work with him. So most of us left along with our drivers."

The show went on the next day as France waived practically all rules in order to assemble enough cars for a field. Little-known Richard Brickhouse won the race in a needle-nosed Dodge Daytona. "No promoter would ever be able to pull off a deal like that nowadays," says Junior, shaking his head.

"There was hard feelings about what happened at Talladega in '69 among some people for a while. Not me. In fact, I took my car and LeeRoy back down there a couple weeks later to test tires for Goodyear. They still couldn't get anything to work. The treads were coming off of 'em. I saw four 'slicks,' treadless tires, that Goodyear had

a-layin' there. I don't know why they even brought them. I said, 'Bolt them things on the car.' The Goodyear guys said there was no point in it, 'cause the rules required treaded tires. I said, if slicks will work here, France will approve 'em. He's got to have a tire that's safe and will last.' The slicks worked. They got a little hot, but Goodyear could easily solve this problem. This is how NASCAR finally came to start using treadless tires."

In the fall of 1969 the Yarbrough-Johnson team scored a somewhat anti-climactic victory in the American 500 at North Carolina Motor Speedway, the seventh win of the season. Although starting only thirty of the year's fifty-four races, the Holly Farms team won $193,611, second only to champion Pearson's $229,760.

Yarbrough was named Ford's man of the year at a festive party in Detroit. Asked to assess LeeRoy as a driver, a rival who requested anonymity thought a few seconds and said, "You could put his brains in your watch pocket, but you couldn't put his courage in a dump truck."

Crew chief Nab paid Yarbrough the ultimate compliment. "I think LeeRoy drives closer to the way Junior did than anybody I've ever seen," declared Nab. "He does it the way Junior likes to see it done."

In 1970 Yarbrough ran just seventeen races for Junior and won only the National 500 at Charlotte that appeared to belong to Bobby Isaac. Shortly after passing Yarbrough for the lead with fourteen laps to go, the engine failed in Isaac's Dodge. LeeRoy then outran Bobby Allison to the finish. It was his tenth, and final, victory with Junior.

In 1971 Yarbrough started just four races for Johnson, posting a best finish of fourth. Then he was gone in a sad, tragic tailspin.

"LeeRoy got it in his head that he wanted to try forms of racing other than NASCAR," says Junior. "He wanted to drive Indy 500–type Champ cars and even the Can-Am roadracing series. I think he might have made a go of it in the Indy cars if he hadn't encountered such bad luck. He had the first race ever run at Ontario Speedway in California won until his engine failed with just a few laps to go.

"In April of '70 we were running a tire test at Texas World Speedway and LeeRoy crashed in the third turn. He hit the wall awful hard and was knocked out for about an hour. The doctors said he was OK, but I'm sure he suffered a concussion. In '71 he got knocked out again when he crashed one of Dan Gurney's cars at Indianapolis. He was hurt very bad this time. A bit after this LeeRoy came down with what we were told was Rocky Mountain Spotted Fever. I've heard other things, like he was abusing painkillers and stuff like that. Whatever it was, he went down pretty fast."

In February of 1980 Yarbrough was charged in Jacksonville, Florida, with trying to strangle his mother, Minnie, with whom he lived. A month later he was ruled incompetent to stand trial and in August was acquitted by reason of insanity.

Junior, concerned and upset by LeeRoy's condition, paid for Yarbrough to be examined at two different psychiatric hospitals in North Carolina. "If they could have helped LeeRoy, I was going to give him a job at our race shop and provide him a place to live," says Junior. "They examined him very thoroughly at both hospitals and came up with the same diagnosis—no hope.

"It was a heartbreaking situation. He could remember everything up to '70. After that, nothing. I'd go to see him at the hospitals and he'd say, 'Where are we racing today? Darlington? Charlotte?' It was tough to handle." In early December of 1984, while the leading figures of NASCAR racing were gathered in New York for a post-season awards program, LeeRoy Yarbrough died in Jacksonville after suffering a seizure at a state mental hospital. He was forty-six.

"People should always have a respect for LeeRoy," says Junior. "He was one of the best prospects to be a superstar when he first buckled in that ever has come along. If his car would run, no one would outrun him, I don't care who it was. He'd have been among our greats if he hadn't been so unlucky to hit the wall a time or two too many."

At the Volunteer 500 at Bristol in July, 1970, the heat was so overwhelming that Donnie Allison was called on to relieve Yarbrough. Allison finished second in the race, two laps behind Dave Marcis, who earlier had relieved Donnie's brother, Bobby. Junior works as gas man during a pit stop in the race. (Dozier Mobley)

81

# CHAPTER NINE

After the lackluster season of 1970 with LeeRoy Yarbrough, Junior was at loose ends. Ford's withdrawal from NASCAR racing had transformed him from a team owner at the summit to a man with no team to own.

At the start of the 1971 season, Yarbrough had entered the Daytona 500 and the Carolina 500 at North Carolina Motor Speedway, which were his final two appearances in cars owned by Junior—1969 Mercuries.

Afterward, Junior used his facilities to build cars and motors to sell to other competitors. For a man who had tasted glory only a couple years earlier, it was a mundane existence. But it didn't last long.

He realized the only way he was going to be able to get back into racing was to acquire the necessary sponsorship. When he learned the tobacco companies had been prohibited from advertising on television by the government, the seeds of a terrific idea were planted in Junior's head.

He contacted R.J. Reynolds Tobacco Company, headquartered in Winston-Salem.

## "It would turn out to be something good."

Above right: Without a sponsor after the 1970 season, Junior targeted tobacco company R.J. Reynolds as a prospect because of their recent prohibition from advertising on television. Junior soon realized that Reynolds's sponsorship potential eclipsed his team's needs. Junior introduced the company to Bill France Sr. and paved the way for their sponsorship of the entire Grand National series. Here, John Marcum, then president of the Automobile Racing Club of America, interviews Junior and Reynolds' first NASCAR liaison, Ralph Seagraves. (Southern MotoRacing)

Opposite: Glotzbach (right) and Junior speak with a NASCAR official during the 1971 season. Junior's new Chevy proved a success and Glotzbach ended up running it thirteen times, scoring one victory at the Volunteer 500 in Bristol, Tennessee. (Pal Parker)

Junior works with Bobby Anderson, Roger Gregory, and Herb Nab (far right) to lower the engine into a new Chevrolet Monte Carlo in preparation for the 1971 World 600 in Charlotte. Junior got the chance to compete again when Howard put up the money for him to build the car that would re-introduce Chevrolet to stock car racing. Driver Charlie Glotzbach is shown in the photo inset. (NASCAR Winston Cup Scene Archives)

"As quick as I could get a meeting with R.J. Reynolds after they left television, that's when I wanted it," Junior says. "I started talking to them late in 1970, and it wasn't until early 1971 that I finally got in to have a meeting with them."

Although it took a while to set up an appointment, Reynolds was intrigued by Junior's proposal to become involved in NASCAR.

"If I had clicked with the right deal and kept my mouth shut, I would have gotten a sponsorship deal with Reynolds for 1971," Junior says. "But they started saying that they had so very much money to spend and so on, that it hit me that they needed to do more in racing than just sponsor a race car, mine or anyone else's."

Junior felt Reynolds needed to talk to Bill France Sr. He called and told him Reynolds would be in touch.

"I realized that once they got together, well, with the way the sport of racing was itching to take off and with the money Reynolds could put behind it, it would turn out to be something good," Junior says.

After negotiations with France, R.J. Reynolds became the series sponsor for the Grand National circuit through its Winston brand of cigarettes in 1971. Winston posted $100,000 in year-end bonus money. Company officials made it clear they intended the new Winston Cup Series to consist of only high-profile races of 250 miles or more. At the time, the NASCAR Grand National championship tour averaged about fifty-one races per year. So in 1971, races of less than 250 miles were not included in the Winston Cup Series, although points earned in those races counted toward the national championship.

R.J. Reynolds provided the financial lift NASCAR needed at a time when the auto manufacturers were withdrawing their direct support. The company spent money on giant billboards, advertising space in newspapers, and promotional packages with NASCAR and its speedways.

Though Junior had introduced Reynolds as the series sponsor, he still had no financial backing to be in racing himself. That changed when Junior entered into a business relationship with a man named Richard Howard.

Howard was a portly, robust, and jovial man. He built his fortune through the furniture business and other enterprises. He also knew how to find money in sports and was credited with bringing Charlotte Motor Speedway out of bankruptcy and making it financially stable.

Howard knew something about promoting races. He was always trying different ideas to put more people into the grandstands at Charlotte.

Following the 1963 season, Chevrolet was not in Grand National racing. Chrysler and Ford held sway. But the odd thing of it was, Chevrolet was far and away the most popular car in America.

The biggest race on Charlotte's schedule was the World 600, held Memorial Day weekend. As it was the speedway's showcase event, Howard wanted the largest possible attendance. He came up with a gem of an idea: Why not bring Chevrolet back into racing? And why not have Junior Johnson drive it? Howard said publicly that fans would swarm to his race for the chance to see Junior compete in a Chevrolet that was capable of winning.

Because Chevrolet was not racing, it had no stock car racing division nor any engineering, personnel, parts, or pieces lined up to become involved in NASCAR's elite series. If Chevrolet were to return to racing, it would be at an entry level. It would take time and money and offer no guarantee a competitive Chevrolet could be built.

Howard was unfazed.

"Richard called me up and asked me if I wanted to build a Chevrolet to run at Charlotte," Junior says. "He asked me

Junior received much-needed financial backing from the jovial Richard Howard in 1971. Howard had built his fortune in the furniture business. He was an owner of Charlotte Motor Speedway and is credited with revitalizing it through his various race promotions. (Daytona Racing Archives)

Right: Expert fabricator Turkey Minton discusses strategy with Junior. Minton joined chief mechanic Nab and engine specialists Horace Smith, Harold Elliott, and Robert Yates to prepare the new Chevy for the World 600. (Dozier Mobley)

Opposite: Junior checks the engine of the new Chevy after preliminary runs at Charlotte. Driver Charlie Glotzbach ended up putting the car on the pole for the race with a speed of 157.788 mph. (NASCAR Winston Cup Scene Archives)

if I would drive it. I said I wouldn't drive, but then I thought about building one. I paused for a minute and I said, 'Well, I don't know, I'll just have to see what's available.' I just didn't know." Junior started investigating the motor, chassis, and components.

What Junior discovered was that the Monte Carlo, the Chevrolet product most suitable for NASCAR racing, would have a few discrepancies in conforming to the sanctioning body's rules requirements.

The body of the Monte Carlo was so wide its wheelbase had to be reduced. Junior knew that in 1967, the Ford Fairlane had a front suspension system that was built into the body of the car. So to allow it to compete, NASCAR permitted Ford to make a new nose.

"So I met with NASCAR and asked them to let me use the Monte Carlo front snout, but to cut it and pull it in where it fit the wheelbase rule," Junior says.

NASCAR knew the value of Chevrolet's renewed presence.

"They agreed to let me do that."

Junior got help from Chevrolet's Vince Piggins, the head of the high-performance division, who assigned Herb Fishel and Walt Springer to help Junior search for the proper parts for both the motor and the chassis.

"With the combination of the boys working on the engines, myself and others on the chassis, and other good fabricators, it turned out that each part of what was then my company worked on various aspects of the new car and had it ready to race in Charlotte," Junior says.

Many of Junior's assistants at that time have become part of NASCAR lore or gone on to greater glory. They include the late Herb Nab, who served as his chief mechanic, the late Turkey Minton, an expert fabricator, and the late Horace Smith, who, along with Harold Elliott and Robert Yates, worked on engines.

That Junior got a Chevrolet ready to race was something of a minor miracle. Only five weeks had elapsed from the time Howard contacted him on April 8 until the World 600 race day.

Charlie Glotzbach, an Indiana native whose sizable reputation as a stock car driver had earned him the nickname "Chargin' Charlie," and who had fallen to LeeRoy Yarbrough and Junior's gumball strategy in 1969, was given the assignment to drive the Chevrolet at Charlotte. Junior liked Glotzbach's style.

"When I got done with the car, I wasn't really sure how it would run. It was all brand new. Everything I had done to it was untried," Junior says.

Shakedown runs a week before the race indicated Junior's new, white No. 3 Chevrolet would be competitive.

"When we showed up at Charlotte, I was shocked and amazed at how fast that car ran," he says. "But then, I knew that having a fast car was kinda Turkey's and Herb's and my cup of tea. Being a driver in the past, I knew what to do, and so did Herb, and so did Turkey. We were fooling with something that was a shot in the dark. So we duplicated every best part of everything we knew."

Glotzbach won the pole position with a speed of 157.788 MPH. From there, he went on to lead the 600-mile race four times for 87 laps and put a lap on the field before lap 234, when he swerved to miss Speedy Thompson on the front stretch and crashed into the wall. Glotzbach wound up twenty-eighth.

Bobby Allison, driving a Mercury for Holman-Moody, won the race.

To the many Chevrolet fans who, as Howard had predicted, came to watch the World 600, it was a disappointment. The race attendance was announced at 78,000. Junior and Howard knew they had something big.

"I was told by the Chevrolet people that the engine wouldn't last, so I had to see how far it would go. I was gonna run it until it blew. Turns out there wasn't anything wrong with the engine."

Howard announced immediately after the race that he would commission Junior to build another Chevrolet for the second Charlotte race, the National 500, in the fall.

They discussed how they might be able to recoup the money they had invested in the development of the Chevrolet. Their car was capable of winning races, they reasoned. Certainly it was much stronger than any of the few Chevrolets being run by independent drivers, and the names Howard, Johnson, and Glotzbach carried a significant amount of clout.

They would offer to race the car at other events if the promoters would pay $10,000 in appearance money.

"That seemed like a lot of money, but as the year went on, it proved so successful for us and the promoters that the promoters started looking at it in a different light," Junior says. "I think they soon realized that it was costing them $10,000 to get us, and they reasoned they could probably get as many as eight to ten other top teams for around $2,000 to $3,000 apiece. That made sense."

Junior and Howard's asking price of $10,000 and the subsequent boost in attendance that their Chevrolet's presence provided gave promoters the incentive to pay money for other elite teams and drivers. This was the foundation for what became the "Winner's Circle" plan, which provided automatic appearance money for teams that won races.

Not all the promoters bit at first.

At a meeting with France and promoters in Daytona, many decided not to take the deal. One, Paul Sawyer at Richmond International Raceway, told Junior he was not interested.

"Later, after the car began doing so well and people were just hanging off the fences to see it, he called me and said he wanted me to bring the car to his race," Junior says. "I said something like, 'You didn't want it the first time I asked, so I'm not bringing it now.' "

As it turned out, Junior relented and the Chevrolet was at Richmond's second race of the season.

After Charlotte, the next race for Glotzbach and the Chevrolet was the Firecracker 400 at Daytona International Speedway on July 4. The Chevrolet withdrew with engine problems after just forty-three laps.

Junior says: "The engine we used was the same one we had used at Charlotte. I was told by the Chevrolet people that the engine wouldn't last, so I had to see how far it would go. I was gonna run it until it blew. Turns out there wasn't anything wrong with the engine, even with all the miles we put on it. It was the fuel pump. So we had a good idea of the engine's limits."

In only its third appearance, the Chevrolet, with Glotzbach behind the wheel, was a winner. With Friday Hassler serving as relief driver for almost half the Volunteer 500 at the 0.533-mile Bristol International Speedway in Bristol, Tennessee, the Chevrolet roared to victory over Bobby Allison by a whopping three laps.

In all, Junior's car led 411 laps and became the first Chevrolet to win a race since Allison won in Islip, New York, on July 7, 1968.

"I said at the time that if we got to winning races, why, the fee for having the Chevrolet would go down," Junior says.

The price never went down, but it didn't seem to inhibit the promoters. Glotzbach ran ten more races for Howard and Junior in 1971, and although he didn't win again, he did have runner-up finishes at Dover, Delaware, in October and North Wilkesboro, North Carolina, in November.

Glotzbach competed in nineteen races in 1971, thirteen of them in the Chevrolet. His lone victory, all seven of his top-five finishes, and all but three of ten appearances among the top ten were earned in the car prepared in Ingles Hollow.

Glotzbach (3) and Bobby Allison (12) battle during the early laps of the World 600 in 1971. Glotzbach would crash on lap 234, finishing a disappointing twenty-eighth. Allison would go on to victory in the Holman-Moody 1969 Mercury. (Don Hunter)

Junior (far left) watches as the crew works on the No. 3 Chevy during a pit stop in the Talladega 500. Glotzbach started third in the race but experienced engine trouble, causing him to finish 33 laps off the pace and in twenty-third place. Bobby Allison won the race. (Pal Parker)

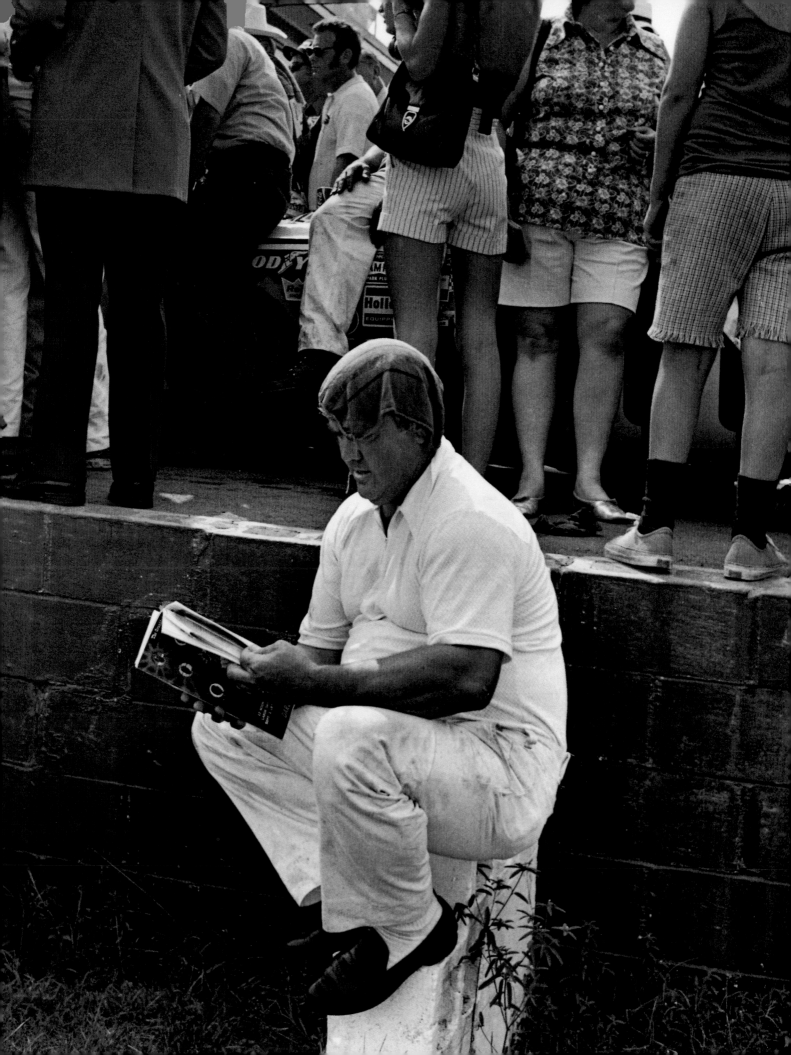

# CHAPTER TEN

In 1972, NASCAR underwent perhaps the most dramatic changes in its history up to that time. All thirty-one races would count toward the Winston Cup Grand National championship.

Bill France Jr. succeeded his father as NASCAR's president on January 11. The point system was overhauled. Races of 400 miles or more awarded 150 points to win with a drop of 3 points per position. The 250-milers carried 100 points to win with a drop of 2 points, and the 100 to 125 milers (of which there were none) offered 50 points to win with a drop of 1 point. This shift emphasized miles completed rather than wins.

The remaining direct factory support ended when Chrysler announced it was pulling out of NASCAR. Without manufacturers, sponsorship money became increasingly important. Petty found it with STP. Nord Krauskopf, with 1970 champion Bobby Isaac as his driver, had K&K Insurance. A.J. Foyt, followed by David Pearson, was with the Wood Brothers, who had Purolator. Veteran team owner Bud Moore came back to NASCAR after a successful stint in Trans-Am racing and ran several drivers during the course of the year.

## "Bobby had a sponsor and Charlie didn't."

Above right: Allison won his first race for Junior at the Atlanta 500 in March 1972. "Bobby was a sly, cagey driver. Whenever he could lead a race, he did. But more times I'd see him stalk someone else and just hunt him down, then go on and pass him," Junior says. (Pal Parker)

Opposite: Junior leafs through the race program while taking a rest outside Victory Lane at Darlington after Allison won the Southern 500. Junior had not been to Victory Lane at Darlington since he was behind the wheel of the winning car in 1965. (Don Hunter)

Bobby Allison's 1972 Chevrolet remains one of the most distinctive cars in NASCAR history. With a red body, white numbers, gold roof, and the familiar Coca-Cola logos, it was hard to miss on the track. (Pal Parker)

Krauskopf (Dodge), Petty (Plymouth), Moore (Ford), and Howard (Chevrolet) received, through NASCAR, extra money for every race they entered. This incentive ensured that the most competitive teams and major brands of cars would be in as many races as possible.

These changes affected how every team prepared for the season.

Junior and Howard began to formulate plans to compete on the entire Winston Cup Grand National schedule in a bid to win the championship and the lucrative bonus from R.J. Reynolds.

With the new shortened schedule in place, many more drivers would participate in every race, which meant promoters would be largely relieved of having to pay to get the stars.

Junior and Howard considered continuing to peddle the Chevrolet for $10,000 a race but realized it might prove more profitable to find a sponsor and race for the championship. Certainly their Chevrolet was capable of winning a title.

But who would drive it?

Junior didn't want to drop Glotzbach, but economics dictated he do so.

"Richard and I were running the Chevrolet for what we could get the tracks to give us for show money," Junior says. "At the same time, there was a driver who had been running for Holman-Moody, and we couldn't help but notice him."

The driver Junior and Howard and virtually everyone else had noticed was Bobby Allison.

Allison was a native Floridian who had relocated to Alabama because stock car racing was plentiful there. He had been successful at several levels of NASCAR competition, but his success on the Grand National circuit had been sporadic, largely because he moved from team to

team and hadn't found the stability that had benefited rivals such as Richard Petty and David Pearson. That changed in 1971 when Allison joined the distinguished Holman-Moody organization as Pearson's replacement.

Holman-Moody was the skilled, high-profile operation Allison needed to display his talent. The statistics tell the story—with the team he won eleven races, including a string of five in a row, and was second only to Petty (twenty-one wins) in season victories. He finished twenty-seven times among the top five and thirty-one among the top ten. He earned $254,316, which made him second to Petty—again—in season earnings. Petty won the 1971 championship with Allison fourth in the final point standings. Allison had made four fewer starts than Petty, forty-two to Petty's forty-six.

At the end of 1971, Holman-Moody folded its operation, which cut Allison loose.

Junior and Howard turned their eyes toward Allison. He had the skill and determination it took to win races, and he also had something else that was critical—$80,000 in sponsorship money from Coca-Cola.

"We talked to him at Rockingham near the end of the season," Junior says. "We needed sponsorship. We needed a full-time driver. Bobby had Coca-Cola as his sponsor. Charlie didn't have anything. It wasn't that we were trying to dump Charlie; it was just that Bobby had a sponsor and Charlie didn't. It was that simple."

Junior felt his Chevrolet would be very competitive for two reasons: first, Allison's driving skill, and second, the car itself. He had taken the basic Chevrolet motor parts and refashioned them to a point where, according to Junior, the engine was "bullet-proof."

"Although a lot of the parts the Chevrolet teams used had looked the same, they weren't," Junior says. "I took

From left to right, crew members Fred Johnson, Nab, Turkey Minton, and Bobby Anderson join Ms. S-K tools on pit road during 1972. The crew's pants, checkered with red-and-white Coca-Cola logos, were as popular as Allison's driving during the season. (Pal Parker)

Allison makes a pit stop during the Southern 500. The toll taken by the demanding racetrack can be seen in Allison's shredded left front tire in the foreground. He won by four car lengths over David Pearson, whom he passed for the lead only six laps from the finish. After the race Pearson said, "I just flat got my fanny outrun." (Southern MotoRacing)

**"I used lighter stuff and did a lot of work on most of the motor pieces myself. So although every Chevrolet motor looked the same, nobody had the same stuff I had. "**

everything out of the motor and had it all remade out of better metal. I used lighter stuff and did a lot of work on most of the motor pieces myself. So although every Chevrolet motor looked the same, nobody had the same stuff I had. My motors and chassis were literally custom-made."

Though it was made by Junior, NASCAR determined the custom fabrication was within the rules.

The Chevrolet Allison drove in 1972 was colorful and remains one of the most distinctive cars in NASCAR's history. It had a red body with white numbers and a gold roof. It was emblazoned with the No. 12 and the familiar Coca-Cola logos. Crew uniforms were white with pants so checkered with the red Coca-Cola logo they weren't too far removed from what Ringling Brothers' clowns might wear.

Junior and Allison wanted badly to win the championship and knock Petty, the 1971 champ, off the throne. The season's tone was set at the first race, the Winston Western 500 on the road course at Riverside, California, on January 23. Petty pulled away from Allison, who had led 100 laps before a faulty valve spring slowed him after 149 of the planned 191 laps. The race was stopped due to dense fog with Petty finishing first and Allison second, the only drivers to complete 149 laps.

It was a good start. Foyt swept away the competition with a win in the Daytona 500. Then at the next race, Richmond, it was again Petty first, Allison second. Allison finished second again in the season's fourth race, the Miller High Life 500 at Ontario, California, then wound up a disappointing twenty-seventh in the fifth race, the Carolina 500 at Rockingham.

If it appeared to some that the Allison-driven Chevrolet wasn't meeting its potential, Junior wasn't concerned. Allison had managed to lead every race. Twice he had been hampered by mechanical problems. Twice more he had finished second.

Also, Junior quickly assessed Allison's style. He didn't manhandle a car to the point where it could no longer function. He simply didn't punish it. And even if it didn't perform as well as it should, Allison got the most out of it. Junior liked that.

"Bobby was a sly, cagey driver," Junior says. "Whenever he could lead a race, he did. But more times, I'd see him stalk someone else and just hunt him down, then go on and pass him. It was like whatever obstacle there was in front of him, he'd do his best to get around it. I knew it was just a matter of time."

That time came in the sixth race of the year, on March 26, and with the style Junior admired. In the Atlanta 500, Allison was a distant third on a restart on lap 268 of the race's 328 laps. He was 7 seconds behind Isaac and Foyt, and there were just thirty laps left.

Foyt wrestled the lead away from Isaac with twelve laps remaining. With five to go, Allison, who had moved up steadily and tenaciously while Foyt fought Isaac for the lead, ducked under Isaac to move into second place. On the next lap, he made the pass around Foyt and went on to win by a mere 0.16 seconds.

It was a thrilling, dramatic victory, and it was the first for a Chevrolet on a superspeedway since Junior himself had won the National 500 at Charlotte on October 13, 1963. The fans knew what they had seen. "Chevy's back!" was their enthusiastic cry. Female patrons lucky enough to have seats in the VIP suites took out lipstick and wrote "Chevy's back!" on the windows.

Although Junior had won a race with Chevrolet and Glotzbach a year earlier, Allison's victory drove the return of Chevy into the public consciousness for two reasons. The car was competing the full schedule as one of the top marques in NASCAR for the first time in a decade,

and it had won a major superspeedway race in front of 50,000 people.

It was fortuitous that Junior had made another improvement to the car. After Allison experienced engine problems at Riverside, Daytona, and Rockingham earlier, Junior had noticed ash droppings on several parts each time the engines were torn down.

"I figured the oil was to blame," Junior says. "So we came up with the idea of avoiding the Union 76 motor oil they gave us at the tracks and went instead with Union's aviation oil, which stood a much higher chance of not breaking down and offered much better protection."

Allison followed his Atlanta triumph with another at Bristol two weeks later. He won again in June at Dover, Delaware, and then three times in succession—at Bristol, Trenton, and again at Atlanta—in July. He had won six races through August 20. Petty, meanwhile, had won five. It was clear the championship was going to be decided between these two drivers.

Allison and Petty waged war on the short tracks, where one could rub, nudge, clip, or just plain slam the other in an effort to gain an advantage—or a victory.

It started calmly on August 27 at Nashville, Tennessee, where Allison won after Petty was blackflagged for ignoring the stop sign on pit road. Petty, enraged by NASCAR's call, lost by ten car lengths as Allison picked up his seventh win of the season. Everything was looking good for Junior's Chevrolet after Allison won his eighth race, the venerated Southern 500 at Darlington on Labor Day.

By the time the circuit reached the half-mile Richmond Fairgrounds Raceway on September 9, there were no other contenders for the championship except Allison and Petty. On the 392nd of the race's 500 laps, Petty, in his red-and-blue Plymouth, passed Allison for the lead. Moments later, Petty's car slid sideways along the top of the guard-rail, then dropped off and bounced back onto the track, still in the lead. He went on to beat Allison.

For Petty, short-track victory No. 1. After the race, both drivers complained of the rough driving, but both said there was no feud.

Two races later, the circuit moved to another short track, the half-miler at Martinsville, Virginia. Junior's Chevrolet was dominant. It won the pole and led 432 of 500 laps. At one point, the car was just a car length from putting Petty's Plymouth, which required an extra pit stop to replace a flat tire, one lap down.

Allison later contended that as he pursued Petty, his rival repeatedly ignored the blue flag that signaled him to move over. Had Petty obeyed it, he would have gone a lap down. As it evolved, a late caution flag allowed Petty to remain on the lead lap and move to Allison's rear bumper on the restart.

The final fifty miles brought the crowd to its feet. At one point, Petty tried to pass on the inside, hit the curb, and whacked Allison's Chevrolet, jarring loose the gas cap.

Noticing the dangling gas cap, NASCAR black-flagged Allison, who paid the flag no heed. Then came another caution flag, which allowed Allison to pit the Chevrolet without penalty.

In the closing laps Allison sideswiped another car, which creased his left rear fender and cut into the tire. With the Chevrolet hampered by the slightly cut tire, it wasn't difficult for Petty to make the pass on lap 462. Allison pressed on until his deflating tire caused him to swerve into Ed Negre. Negre's Dodge went into the wall. Petty went on to win by 6 seconds over Allison.

For Petty, short-track victory No. 2.

After the race, Allison was fined $500 by NASCAR for ignoring the black flag. He also had to pay for repairing the damage to Negre's car. Not surprisingly, Allison was angry and questioned why he was fined when Petty hadn't been for ignoring the blue flag at Martinsville. Still, Allison and Petty refused to admit there was a feud.

Junior didn't buy that.

"I believe that Bobby was a little hard-headed," Junior says today. "But I also believe that at that time, he really resented Richard outrunning him. I think Bobby tried to knock Richard out and save his car but it looked to me that it went the other way. Richard would knock Bobby out whether he went on to win the race or not."

Junior never counseled Allison to back off. He knew Allison was doing the best he could to win races and take the measure of Petty. He knew Allison wasn't going to back down from any challenge.

The final short-track race of the year came on October 1 at North Wilkesboro Speedway, the twenty-eighth of the season's thirty-one races.

*At North Wilkesboro, Allison passed Richard Petty out of turn four with only three laps to go, but not before the two cars came together and crashed into the wall. Both cars continued racing, with Allison dealing with a smoke-filled interior and Petty a badly dented front left fender. In the next turn Petty retook the lead after another collision and sped to victory. (Daytona Racing Archives)*

On lap 397, Allison ducked under Petty in an attempt to take the lead. Petty sliced low to cut Allison off and did so successfully by using the car of rookie Vic Parsons as a blocker. As Petty made the move, he and Allison locked up and crashed into the wall together.

They separated and Allison took the lead, with Petty in close pursuit. The two went into the first turn side by side and slammed into the wall again. Somehow, they moved apart to complete the final two laps. Petty beat Allison by two car lengths.

For Petty, short-track win No. 3.

But Petty was not happy. "He could have put me in the boondocks," he said of Allison. "There's not going to be any

more trouble until he hurts somebody. If he does that, there is going to be real trouble. He's playing with my life out there. That I don't like."

Meanwhile, Allison, hot, tired, and with a cold towel wrapped around his neck, sat quietly atop a flatbed truck in the infield. Swarms of Allison and Chevrolet loyalists congregated around him. Some angry fans suggested they confront the Pettys as a group, not unlike a lynch mob.

"No, no, we're not going to have any of that," Allison quietly said, shaking his head.

"He had to wreck me in order to win, and that's what he did," Allison said. "I had so much smoke in my car I could hardly see."

As Petty took part in the Victory Lane ceremonies, an intoxicated fan hurdled the fence and attacked him. He was repelled by a whack over the head from Petty's helmet, delivered by Maurice Petty, Richard's brother.

"You never really know who hit who first or for what reason," Junior says. "I never got in the middle of it. I've seen two or three occasions where, I think, certain people have been more mad at the car than they were the driver, so they want to take out the car. I think Bobby looked at Richard's car in that light. I think he resented that car."

Allison said years later, "The only thing I can say about those deals with Richard, the races where we bumped and shoved and such and the ill feelings that arose, is that all of a sudden he felt a threat from me. I don't think he ever raced anyone as tenacious as I was."

Allison won at Charlotte and Rockingham, whereas Petty finished tenth and second, respectively (which granted Allison a measure of revenge), and third to Allison's fourth in the final race of the year at College Station, Texas. Nevertheless, Petty won the championship by 127.90 points.

Many speculated that Allison's three straight short-track losses to Petty cost him the championship. Junior knew there was more to it. From almost the outset of their association, Allison said there was a distinct gap in his communication with Junior. He believed that Junior, for whatever reasons, refused to talk with him directly.

Perhaps he believed that his ideas and suggestions didn't receive their due notice. Allison had made his way in racing largely on his own, and was very adept at building and maintaining racecars. He had his own ideas about how things should be done and what would make a car run better.

Whatever the reason, Allison was convinced he wasn't being heard.

Since then, Allison has said Junior treated him like a ghost. That he could be standing alongside Junior and rather than speak to him directly Junior would turn to chief mechanic Herb Nab and say, "Herb, tell Bobby we need a different set of springs in the car before we test again."

Allison maintains he made repeated attempts to force Junior to communicate with him directly, but Junior would just walk away.

"Junior was very quiet," Allison says in retrospect. "He never let me know what was on his mind to give me the opportunity to take his knowledge. What I would hear from Junior would not be when our ideas agreed and we won but when our ideas disagreed and we won or lost. If our ideas happened to disagree on something and we won, he would still be very unhappy."

As an example, Allison recalls a race in Trenton in which he insisted a Chevrolet chassis, not a modified one, be used. He won the race.

When asked about the well-documented claims of miscommunication, Junior says, "Yeah, I heard where I supposedly never talked to him. I supposedly talked to

Herb and Herb talked to him. That's not true. He'll act like that's the way it was, but if I've got something to say to somebody, I don't talk to anyone else. If I had something to say to Bobby about what he was doing with my car, I would be the first one to tell him."

Junior also felt Allison was not completely committed to the team.

"I am convinced Bobby had every intention of running just one year with me and then forming his own team. Vince Piggins, the head of Chevrolet, was a big damn fan of Bobby's and more or less provided Bobby a way to go with Chevrolet whenever he wanted to do it."

Allison later agreed that part of this was true. "I said then my long-range plan was to drive for Ralph Moody in 1973 [who planned to have his lawsuit with partner John Holman completed by that time], and both Junior and Richard Howard knew that."

During the Winston 500 on May 7, 1972, at Talladega, Junior was further convinced that Allison had his own agenda.

"Where I got crossed up with Bobby was at that race," Junior says. "We were running along in decent shape to win the championship. We had run a handful of laps before we burned up an oil line."

The car started smoking after thirty-four laps because of oil on the exhaust pipes. Allison came into the garage area, and Junior's crew started fixing the oil line so he could get back in the race.

With the new point system designed to reward miles completed, Allison could still return to the track and pile up many more miles and earn vital points.

"It took us just a few laps to fix the oil line," Junior says. "We assumed Bobby would still be around to drive the car.

We started hunting for him and finally someone said, 'Bobby got in his car and went home.' "

At Talladega, Allison finished forty-fifth. Petty, meanwhile, finished fourth. That meant a huge disparity in points between the two.

"I've heard everything he's had to say since—I did this and I treated him this way and that," Junior says. "That's not the way it happened. I'm not going to hug somebody's damn neck who's not going to unify the team and help us win whatever we can win."

How Allison was ultimately released from Howard's team is another example of how he and Junior saw their relationship from polar opposite viewpoints.

Allison says he was in Riverside, California, for a Trans-Am race after the end of the season, when he got a phone call in his motel room at 5 A.M.—8 A.M. North Carolina time. It was Richard Howard. Howard said, "Me and Junior have been talking, and we want to know yes or no: Are you going to drive for us next year? If you're not, we have a chance to get the best driver in NASCAR right now."

To which Allison, not yet fully awake, angrily replied, "Get him." And he hung up.

"Moody's 1973 deal wasn't coming together like it needed to," Allison says. "With Junior, I did feel like I was an asset to his deal and he in turn had enhanced my career tremendously. Coke was willing to once again up the ante. It looked like we'd be able to go racing right along. Then I got that phone call.

"If it had come at noon the same day, I would have probably said, 'Hey, wait a minute.' I would have told them they already had the best one, or however I could have addressed the situation. Anyway, at 10 that same morning, they announced that they had signed Cale Yarborough.

I don't think they started from scratch when they called me. But at the same time, they were aware that I had been conversing with Moody and so forth."

Junior remembers the turning point for him and Howard.

"We were at Rockingham late in the year trying to work the thing out for 1973. Richard and Bobby were sitting in a car talking about driving next year. Bobby said, 'Yeah, I want to drive for you next year, but I want all the sponsorship money and 50 percent of what the car wins.' That's what Richard Howard came back and told me."

That was all Junior needed to hear after his disappointment with Allison at Talladega.

"I said, 'Well, he can have all the sponsorship and half the winnings,'" Junior says. "All he's got to do now is find a damn car to drive."

In the coming years, Bobby would come close to beating Junior's team for the championship, but he ultimately fell short. Today Junior says he understands Bobby's desire to own and race his own car. He had a great opportunity with Chevrolet. Had it succeeded, it would have been great for him.

"But the reason it didn't click in the years after he left me," Junior says, "was that you had Glen Wood sittin' there with David Pearson, you had me sittin' there with Cale Yarborough, you had Richard Petty sittin' there, and those three racing teams dominated the sport for a long, long time after 1972. There wasn't anybody who could crack those three teams, including Bobby.

"If Bobby had stayed with me," Junior says, "I don't think Richard Petty's records today would mean anything. That's the caliber of driver Bobby was. I switched drivers after he left, of course, and our team never seemed to slow up. Not at all. I don't think it would have slowed up at all with Bobby in the car."

# CHAPTER ELEVEN

As a driver, Cale Yarborough was the mirror image of Junior in his prime. He didn't know much about finesse; instead, he was simply fearless and drove a car to its limits and beyond. As a competitor, he was fond of saying that there were only two parts of racing, winning and losing. There was no second place, no third place. When Junior was a driver, he said virtually the same thing.

Yarborough's reputation as a daredevil was forged in his youth, which was a hardscrabble existence in Timmonsville, South Carolina. He had wrestled with an alligator as a kid after falling into a river, been bitten on the toe by a rattlesnake (the snake was found dead the next morning; Yarborough was virtually unfazed), been knocked on his butt by lightning (he got up and walked away), gotten shot (the wound was not serious), fallen out of an airplane (the parachute opened just enough to save his life), compiled an impressive record as a Golden

# "Cale was what we were looking for."

Above right: In 1973 Yarborough found Victory Lane early in his campaign with Junior when he won the season's fifth race, the Southeastern 500 in Bristol, in dominant style. He led all 500 laps of the race and beat Richard Petty by two laps. Herb Nab (far right) and Junior join Yarborough in the post-race celebration. (Pal Parker)

Opposite: Yarborough's fourth and final win of 1973 came in the controversial National 500 at Charlotte Motor Speedway. Yarborough took the checkered flag, with Richard Petty second and Bobby Allison third. Allison protested to NASCAR that Junior and Petty's cars must have had oversized engines. (Don Hunter)

# "I knew Cale was a determined hard charger," Junior says. "Richard and I knew that from his connection with Glen Wood."

Gloves boxer, been a tenacious fullback in semipro football, and nursed a desire to race fast cars by slamming his way around bull rings, where rules and etiquette didn't apply.

There are stories of the young Yarborough hanging on the fences to watch the Southern 500 at Darlington and then sneaking into the pits, only to be chased out by NASCAR officials.

By 1963, he was competing regularly on NASCAR's elite stock car circuit, his life's goal. He drove for various smaller team owners until his reputation as a driver who couldn't tolerate anything but being out front led him to his first significant ride. In 1966, he joined the Wood Brothers team—one of NASCAR's best—and won thirteen races through 1970 driving their Fords. He was an established star.

But like Junior, Yarborough was hurt by Ford's pullout in 1970. Glen Wood said he wasn't sure what direction the team was going to take and simply couldn't assure Yarborough that things would remain the same after Ford's exit.

Yarborough's reputation had spread beyond the Southeast, and he was offered the opportunity by Gene White, a wealthy Firestone Tire distributor, to compete on the United States Auto Club's Indy Car circuit. That was far removed from the stock cars in which Yarborough had experienced all his success. But it would mean he would get the chance to compete in the Indianapolis 500, the greatest sporting event in the world and considered by most race drivers at that time to be the highest level of competition.

For Yarborough, Indy Car racing was a disaster. During the two years he spent with White, he competed in twelve races with only a pair of top-five finishes in 1971. Then in 1972, White cut his team from two cars to one, and

Yarborough was without a ride. For all of 1972, he drove only in the Indianapolis 500 and made five NASCAR starts in his own car.

He was miserable. He said that leaving NASCAR was the biggest mistake he had ever made.

"I knew Cale was a determined hard charger," Junior says. "Richard and I knew that from his connection with Glen Wood. LeeRoy had been with us but unfortunately he got sick. We lost him. Then we had Bobby, and with those two men, we had kinda gotten used to the caliber of drivers they were. We didn't want anything else."

When weighing his decision, Junior had to compare Bobby's obvious skills with the gutsy style of Cale.

"At the time, Cale was what we were looking for. Now, whether we could tie him to the ground and get out of him what we could get out of him, we didn't know."

Yarborough joined Junior's team before the 1973 season.

During the years 1973 through 1975, NASCAR was in flux. There were so many controversial changes that it seemed the sanctioning body had no real sense of direction.

The points system changed twice. Rules were altered almost constantly. The energy shortage of 1974 threatened racing's very existence. Teams scrapped for sponsorship, and those without it fell by the wayside, which diminished the quality of the sport. NASCAR responded to this, and the surging rebellion by drivers bitter over their lack of income, by offering various programs to grant appearance money to selected teams. Teams were accused of cheating. NASCAR was accused of letting the cheating teams get away with it.

In spite of the oft-frustrating transitions within NASCAR during much of the early 1970s, Junior says today that it was all fun. He readily admits the eight years he spent with Yarborough, the short, stocky, barrel-chested

Junior and Richard Howard decided in 1973 on Cale Yarborough as their driver. Yarborough, seated in the car, was known as a daredevil on and off the racetrack. In his youth he wrestled an alligator and compiled a respectable record as a Golden Gloves boxer. (Don Hunter)

driver, rank among the most enjoyable of his tenure in motorsports.

"With us, Cale took the sport to a higher level," Junior says. "It was refreshing to see us do what we did without the factory backing. That was perhaps the biggest thing, that we all had to do it on our own—get the sponsors if we could, and go out there and race."

The trek to the higher level began in 1973, when Yarborough remarkably led all 500 laps of the Southeastern 500 at Bristol on March 25, the fifth race of the season, to win his first race with Junior. He finished two laps ahead of Richard Petty on the 0.533-mile track. After his victory, Yarborough said he had never had an easier, smoother ride. For him, the race was like a Sunday drive.

Three more victories followed. On May 12, Yarborough won his second race, on the half-miler at Nashville. He finished two laps up on Benny Parsons. Fittingly, Yarborough's next victory was in the Southern 500 at Darlington, the track near his home that had entranced him as a youngster. Yarborough's fourth and final win of the year came on October 7 in the National 500 at Charlotte Motor Speedway. It was one of the most controversial races in NASCAR's history and is a perfect example of how the sanctioning body often seemed at loose ends during the early '70s.

Yarborough had won by 1.4 seconds over Petty. Both were two laps ahead of the third-place driver, Bobby Allison, who drove his own Chevrolet—as Junior had predicted—sponsored by Coca-Cola. Allison was "curious" as to how the cars of Yarborough and Petty could put six to eight car lengths on him down the straightaways of the 1.5-mile Charlotte track and immediately sought out chief inspector Bill Gazaway.

He posted $200 in protest money and accused Junior's Chevrolet and Petty's Dodge of having oversized engines.

NASCAR refused Allison's protest money. Perhaps it did not want to admit he had a complaint. Instead, it ordered an engine tear-down of the top-three finishing cars. Post-race inspections were not the norm in NASCAR, as they are today.

Allison's car was rolled out of the inspection first, declared legal by Gazaway.

Hours passed, and neither Junior's Chevrolet nor Petty's Dodge left the inspection area. The situation was tense. Howard fumed. He claimed Junior's Chevrolet had passed prerace inspection and then, six hours later, NASCAR couldn't determine if the car was legal. He contended that as the race promoter, he had been paying the inspectors to be at his track all week, and if some illegal cars got by them, he had wasted his money. He also said that if the order of finish was changed, he was going to drag NASCAR into court.

It was after 10 P.M. when Gazaway said that the measurements of the engines in Yarborough's, Petty's, and Allison's cars would be sent to NASCAR headquarters in Daytona Beach—even though Allison's car was declared legal—and that a final determination would be made on Monday, October 8.

At 5 P.M. on Monday, twenty-five hours after the conclusion of the race, NASCAR ruled that Yarborough's victory was official. The sanctioning body said the procedure used to check the engines in Charlotte was inadequate. Because the prerace inspection procedures had determined that the cars conformed to the rules, the results of the race were official.

Allison was furious. He claimed NASCAR had done nothing more than figure a way to lie out of the situation,

Junior tosses away an empty gas can and reaches for a replacement from crew member (and future team owner) Robert Yates during a pit stop in 1973. Yarborough finished the year second in the championship race, 67.15 points behind Benny Parsons. (Pal Parker)

knowing full well the engines were illegal. He threatened to quit NASCAR and withdrew from the next race, the American 500 at Rockingham.

Three days later, Allison announced he was suing NASCAR. He claimed it had stolen money from him by allowing illegal cars that NASCAR had deemed legal to finish ahead of his.

Allison's actions drew national attention. Meanwhile, NASCAR President Bill France Jr. remained unavailable for comment. It wasn't until the two men met in Atlanta on October 15 that the situation was resolved. It was announced that Allison would compete at Rockingham, and that Allison had expressed confidence that NASCAR would take steps to avoid misunderstandings about rules and penalties in the future. Additionally, NASCAR would study its inspection procedures and, at Rockingham, would institute a post-race inspection to check carburetor plates, air cleaners, and engine size.

Allison never said whether he received any financial compensation. He said only that he was satisfied. Years later he said he never received a dime.

The whole thing was a mess.

It did no good for NASCAR. And it did no good for Yarborough and Junior. Regardless of the official outcome, the victory was tainted because of the post-race controversy. Junior swore his Chevrolet's engine was not oversized. If he was going to cheat, he said, he'd want cheating to be worthwhile and would run an engine sized no less than 500 cubic inches (73 cubic inches larger than legal).

Junior maintains today that his engine was legal and that, indeed, NASCAR's inspection methods *were* insufficient to do a precise job. "All my engine guys were concerned with was our own car," Junior says. "What somebody's got and what NASCAR says he's got always creates some kind of

conflict. NASCAR just didn't have the right kind of measuring equipment you really needed to pinpoint if an engine was legal or if it wasn't legal. If it was 2 or 3 cubic inches one way or the other, why, it was so iffy."

Junior explains that NASCAR's procedure was to measure total engine displacement by measuring one cylinder then multiplying by eight. At the time, his engines had as many small cylinders as it did big ones—bigger by two or three-thousandths of a cubic inch.

"That confused a lot of engine builders, and it confused inspectors, to the point that they could very easily disqualify you for having a 430-cubic-inch engine versus a 427-cubic-inch engine or whatever size they were at the time," Junior says. "But if you measured them all individually, then you had an engine in the legal limits."

By year's end, Yarborough had been everything Junior thought he would be. He won four races, second among all competitors that year (David Pearson scorched the superspeedways with eleven wins) and finished second to Benny Parsons in the final point standings. More importantly, Yarborough earned $267,513, more than any driver that season. That was crucial because team sponsorship and winnings paid the bills rather than Detroit manufacturers.

The most significant thing that happened during the next season, 1974, was that for the first time in his career, Junior expanded to a two-car operation. Carling Brewing Company had spent the first part of the season backing rookie Earl Ross, a Canadian, with a smaller team. Eager to gain a bigger foothold in NASCAR, Carling decided it would sponsor Junior's team, which would provide a second car for Ross. Carling's support was for the remainder of 1974 and for the first part of 1975, with options for three more years.

In fact, Carling bought the assets of Junior Johnson & Associates because it wanted to establish a Canadian team in NASCAR, one run by Canadians, wearing the logos of

Canadian Earl Ross (52) and Yarborough (11) race during the Firecracker 400 at Daytona. In an unusual finish, Yarborough tied with Buddy Baker for third place and Ross finished thirteenth. It would prove to be the best combined race for the Carling team during their short time together. (Daytona Racing Archives)

a Canadian Company. The deal was simply too good for Junior to refuse.

At the time of the announcement, Yarborough was leading the point standings. Petty clinched the championship at Rockingham two weeks before the season's end. Several days later Carling announced it was pulling out of NASCAR—for good. The company had sponsored Johnson for only four months, when it had promised to do so for as many as four years.

Junior was stunned, but he wasn't angry. He liked the Carling people and had worked well with them. What happened was that the people in the United States who had an interest in Carling were bought out by an individual in South Africa, according to Junior. Junior had dealt with the Canadians who supported Ross, but it was the South African ownership that pulled the sponsorship.

What Carling's Canadian division had to do was get Junior to participate in a buyback. At first they offered him a 25 percent buyback, but Junior was too smart for that. He realized that Carling would spend 15 percent of the selling price on freight costs to bring the assets to Canada, which would leave them only 10 percent of their original offer. So he bid 10 percent.

"When the company was pulling out and basically going home to Canada, they started looking into what it cost to get the racing assets back into Canada," Junior recalls. "It just about cost them more to do that than to drop the whole thing and forget about it."

How could Junior be upset with Carling? He had made a profit with the buyback, and Carling's sponsorship and promotional efforts had served his team very well. Ross

Junior and Nab watch from the pits during the Delaware 500 in 1974, where Earl Ross finished third. One month later, after only four months of sponsorship, Carling announced it would not be involved with Grand National racing the following year. (Dozier Mobley)

won the Rookie of the Year title, but he never raced in NASCAR again.

In 1974, Yarborough was able to match eventual champion Petty win for win. Both had won ten times, but one more finish among the top five and top ten for Petty made the difference, and it was a big one. Petty won the title by more than 567 points.

In spite of his strong season, Junior had no sponsorship and no way to pay for the coming year after Carling's pull-out. And Junior refused to use his own money to race.

For 1975 he and Yarborough would have to rely on appearance money to compete when and where they could.

Recognizing that sponsorship dilemmas might keep some of its best teams away from the tracks, NASCAR adopted a policy it hoped would ensure their presence at every race. It selected four teams running four different makes of cars to receive special appearance money. The teams were Petty Enterprises, Bud Moore Engineering (Buddy Baker), K&K Insurance (Dave Marcis) and Junior, with Yarborough. Each would be paid $3,000 per superspeedway race and $2,000 for each short-track event, and were required to run all the races on the series.

Junior declined. He figured the money offered wasn't nearly enough to cover his expenses to compete in every race. Instead he would be selective and negotiate the best deal he could with each track promoter.

By the time the season started, Howard was no longer associated with Junior. He had become locked in a duel for control of Charlotte Motor Speedway with Bruton Smith, co-founder of the track with Curtis Turner in 1960. Smith had left North Carolina after the track went into bankruptcy. He returned—worth millions—with every intention of owning it again.

Howard sold Smith 80,000 shares of his stock, which gave Smith controlling interest, again.

At the start of 1975, Junior had to watch his expenses. He did not enter his Chevrolets in three of the season's first five races because the track promoters wouldn't provide what he thought was appropriate appearance money. Yarborough, however, won in just his second start of the year, in the Carolina 500 at Rockingham on March 2.

After the season's seventh race, at North Wilkesboro, where Yarborough finished second to Petty, Junior got his badly needed sponsorship. Ironically, it came from Holly Farms, the North Wilkesboro–based poultry firm that had been Junior's backer when he began racing full-time in 1960.

"What Holly Farms did for me was good for me, good for them and good for racing," Junior says. "They stuck with racing, and that was very important during a time when sponsors were bouncing off the walls. Holly Farms was one of the best sponsors I ever had."

With Holly Farms aboard (save for one race, in Riverside, California), Yarborough and Junior made a concentrated effort to return to the form they had established in their first two years together.

The championship, however, was out of the question because they missed three early-season races. In fact, the 1975 season was something of a disappointment. Yarborough won only three races in twenty-seven starts and finished a distant ninth in the final point standings. It appeared that even with Holly Farms' sponsorship, Junior's team was slipping, losing the impetus of 1973 that had led to the brilliant 1974.

Junior leans on the jack handle as Henry Benfield and an unidentified crew member watch the action during the 1975 Dixie 500 at Atlanta International Raceway. The team sat out three of the first five races before Holly Farms came through with badly needed sponsorship after a victory in the seventh race. This allowed the team to return to a full schedule. (Dozier Mobley)

The bottle reads: Vintage 1976 / Wilkes County Champagne

# CHAPTER 12

In 1976, Junior and Yarborough reached the pinnacle of stock car racing when they won the Winston Cup championship.

Yarborough won nine times en route to the title, nearly matching his ten-win effort of 1974. This time, however, the difference was consistency. Junior's Chevrolets finished more times among the top five (twenty-two) and the top ten (twenty-three) than any other car in NASCAR.

Yarborough was not the dominant driver of 1976. Pearson, driving for the Wood Brothers, won ten of the twenty-two races he entered.

However, with his limited schedule he was no contender for the championship. "Cale's determination was unbelievable as far as what we could do with the motors, the cars, and stuff of that nature," Junior says. "Cale didn't have to lean on a motor to the point where he tore it up. He didn't have to hang himself out with the car and take a chance on tearing up the various combinations we had. He stayed pretty much in the safety zone most of the time."

Cale's only interests were winning races and winning the championship. Those were the focal points of his determination. He had no hidden agenda, as Junior suspected of Allison.

## "Let 'em kill each other as far as I'm concerned."

Above right: At the Daytona 500, Yarborough made a strong start to the 1977 season, beating Benny Parsons by 1.39 seconds. It was Yarborough's second win in NASCAR's most prestigious race. (Don Hunter)

Opposite: Yarborough offers Junior a jar of Wilkes County Champagne (which of course was moonshine) at the christening of North Wilkesboro Speedway's 2,500-seat Junior Johnson Grandstand on April 4, 1976. That year Yarborough and Junior cruised to the championship by winning nine times and scoring an incredible twenty-two top five finishes, and thirty-three top tens. (Southern MotoRacing)

Left:Junior chats on pit road with presidential candidate Jimmy Carter at Atlanta in March 1976. Carter was governor of Georgia and went on to win the election in November. "Jimmy Carter was a president who put ordinary people on the same level with himself," says Junior. "He was a race fan." (Junior Johnson collection)

Opposite: Junior leans into the jack as Yarborough makes a pit stop. Junior says: "When you have a guy who gives you 100 percent, who will hang the car on the wall every lap if he has to in order to win, then you are able to extend. You extend the motors, the chassis set-ups, the gear arrangements, and so forth. You don't have trouble when you do that." (Dozier Mobley)

"When you have that guy who gives you 100 percent, who will hang the car on the wall every lap if he has to in order to win, then you are able to extend," Junior says. "You extend the motors, the chassis setups, the gear arrangements, and so forth. You don't have trouble when you do that.

"That's what made the difference for us those three years."

It took those three years, Junior says, for his team to function at a championship level and to fully mesh with Yarborough's skills.

"When I lost the 1972 championship with Bobby, it kinda irritated me," Junior says. "That's because I felt like the crew, myself, and everyone else was doing their job to win the championship. The deserved to win it; they worked to win it.

"And when we lost it like we did, I was determined to get back to the point where I had the driver and the team to win the championship. We had our trial-and-error years with Cale, no doubt about that. They were good years, but we still had our share of bad moments.

"When Cale got settled in, he started winning a lot. And our team was put back together. It was put back together to the point where we could dominate the sport for years."

In 1977, Yarborough seized the point lead early and held it through the first seventeen races. Then in July he lost it to Petty after Petty finished second at Pocono and Yarborough finished sixth.

After a second-place finish in the Talladega 500 on August 7, Yarborough complained that Junior's Chevrolet lacked power.

"It was," Yarborough said at the time, "the sorriest Chevrolet in the race. If I had won the race, I would have to be in court Monday morning for stealing."

Junior was not pleased. "Here we are, in the middle of some engine problems right now, and we're in the middle of the championship battle," he said at the time. "If Cale starts running his mouth, he'll be looking for another car. We don't have to listen to a bunch of lip from him."

But Junior and Cale ended up having to deal with lip from someone else during their championship run. Darrell Waltrip was a brash young driver out of Kentucky who landed his 1977 ride with fledgling DiGard Racing. Prior to that year, he had won three short-track races in his career and was itching to show his stuff on the superspeedways. With the DiGard Chevrolet, he had the car to do it.

Waltrip was smart. He knew he had to perform on the track and he had to call attention to himself and his efforts to break up the old guard of winners, including Yarborough. He saw himself as the driver of the future. That prompted him to tweak other drivers' noses. He did it verbally, not unlike the young Muhammad Ali. Whenever an opportunity arose to zing another competitor or thump his own chest, Waltrip took it.

Race fans had never seen, or heard, anything like it. With Waltrip, there was no middle ground. Either he was loved or hated. His rivals, including Yarborough, hated him. However, as Waltrip began to win races, he gained their grudging respect. Not from Yarborough, however.

Yarborough thought so little of Waltrip and his braggadocio that he tagged the young driver with the now-famous nickname, "Jaws," after the vastly popular book and movie about a great white shark.

At the Southern 500 on Labor Day, Waltrip won the pole and then he and Yarborough staged one of the great battles in Darlington history. Waltrip led eleven times, Yarborough nine. With 100 laps to go, they carried their fight into thick traffic. Yarborough passed Waltrip going into the first turn, but Waltrip retook the lead out of the second turn. They headed straight for three lapped cars.

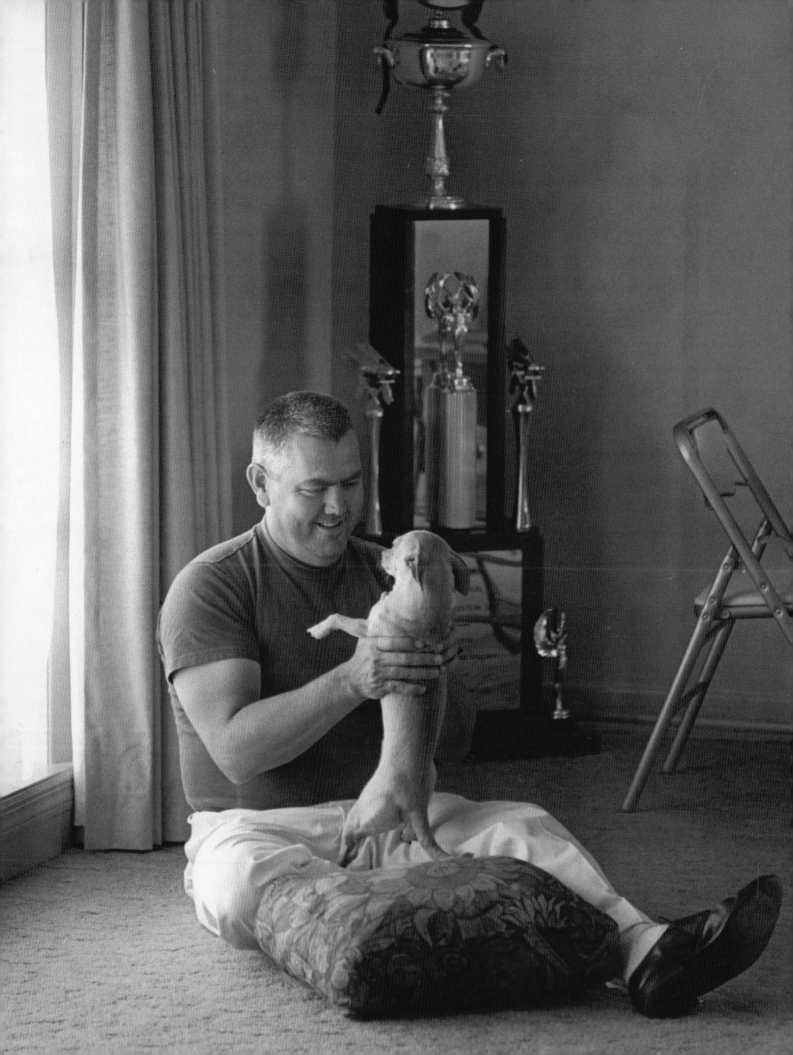

Right: Yarborough makes a pit stop during the Talladega 500 in August. Although he finished second, Yarborough complained to the media that the car lacked power, which prompted Junior to retort, "If Cale starts running his mouth, he'll be looking for another car." (T. Taylor Warren)

Opposite: On January 3, 1976, Junior's dog, Cricket, shown in this 1966 photo, was stolen from Junior's car while he was at a restaurant. After offering a $1,000 reward—no questions asked—Junior got a call from a man who said he had found Cricket running down the street and would return him for the reward. Junior was warned not to contact the law if he wanted Cricket back. He followed the man's rendezvous instructions, paid him, and brought Cricket home. (NASCAR Winston Cup Scene Archives)

Neither backed off. There was a smoking five-car crash in the third turn that seriously damaged both their Chevrolets. They were able to continue racing, with Yarborough finishing fifth and Waltrip sixth.

Afterward, driver D.K. Ulrich, involved in the accident, walked over to Yarborough and asked why he had run all over him.

"I didn't touch you," Yarborough replied. "Jaws hit you."

Ulrich asked just who the hell Jaws was.

"Jaws Waltrip. Ol' Jaws," Yarborough said. "Waltrip hit you and knocked you into the wall. You came off and hit me. It was totally uncalled for."

The media seized the nickname immediately. Jaws was in the headlines.

Three races after Darlington, Yarborough's mouth got him into trouble again, this time with H. Clay Earles, the headstrong promoter at Martinsville Speedway. This gave Waltrip the opportunity for a counterstrike.

Yarborough won the Old Dominion 500 at Martinsville on a very hot and humid September day. Exhausted, he was pulled from his car, and he quickly criticized the 500-lap length of the race. He said it needed to be cut, that driver fatigue was becoming more dangerous than actual racing.

Earles shot back that the length of his races wouldn't be cut and that Yarborough should simply shut up and consider the handsome payoff he got for winning as ample compensation for completing 500 laps.

One race later, Waltrip pounced.

He beat Yarborough at North Wilkesboro, a 0.625-mile track, to earn his fifth win of the season. Remembering Yarborough's complaints about the length of short-track races, he said, "This was about a one-and-a-half to two on the Cale Scale. I think Cale's problem could be his years."

Yarborough was thirty-eight years old, Waltrip thirty. "I know I'm finding out I can't do the same things I could ten years ago," Waltrip continued.

Yarborough, however, could be smug about the whole thing. At North Wilkesboro, Petty had been eliminated in a crash on the 240th of the race's 400 laps. Yarborough's point lead was 293 over Petty and was virtually insurmountable. Yarborough and Junior were locked into their second straight title.

The verbal feud delighted fans and the media. Unlike the on-track, all-out war between Allison and Petty, where car damage and potential injury concerned everyone, this was fun.

At Charlotte in October, some prankster brought to pit road a real shark (dead, of course), which dangled from a tow truck's hook with a chicken—symbolic of Junior's Holly Farms sponsorship—in its mouth.

"It was fun," Junior remembers. "I kinda alluded to Darrell and the mouth he had on him a few times. But around a racetrack, well, it's just the way it is. You get a bunch of guys around and they'll nickname somebody and start jokes and stuff about them and all. Most of the stuff going on between Cale and Darrell was done in a fun way."

Yarborough agrees. "Ol' Jaws?" he says. "Darrell has always been a fierce competitor and a good race driver. We didn't have any problems, although it may have looked like it. I think the fans had more going about us than we did ourselves. Darrell and I were never mad at each other. We just let it ride."

Yarborough won the championship by nearly 400 points over Petty. He won nine times (three on superspeedways and six times in ten short-track races) and had a car that glowed with consistency. With the slope-nosed Chevrolet Laguna on superspeedways and the Monte Carlo on the

Junior and the crew work to repair Yarborough's car after his crash with Waltrip in the 1977 Southern 500. After the race Yarborough would coin the nickname "Jaws" for the talkative and tenacious Waltrip. (T. Taylor Warren)

short tracks, Yarborough compiled twenty-five finishes among the top five and twenty-seven in the top ten. It was a remarkable achievement in a thirty-race season.

The 1978 championship season began with a switch. NASCAR made another rule change that allowed all General Motors cars to run Chevrolet's 350-cubic-inch engine. With that, Junior dropped Chevrolet, the car he had almost single-handedly brought back into NASCAR just six short years earlier. Yarborough would drive Oldsmobiles in 1978.

"The Oldsmobile just looked like it was a better car," Junior says. "We thought its design was more suited for what we wanted. We liked the shape of it. We thought it was the best of the General Motors cars at that particular time."

At first, it appeared everything would be fine. Yarborough won at Riverside, on the road course, in January.

Then problems arose. Yarborough won the pole for the Daytona 500 with a first-lap speed of 187.536 MPH. He skipped his second qualifying lap because he was nervous.

"You wouldn't believe how unstable the car is," Yarborough said. "I don't know what it's going to be like out there with other cars. I'll have to psyche myself up."

He did a good job of it. He finished second to Allison, who was driving Bud Moore's Ford, and was the only other driver to complete all 200 laps around the 2.5-mile Daytona track.

It wasn't until May in the Winston 500 on the 2.66-mile Alabama International Motor Speedway in Talladega that Yarborough won again. He whipped around Buddy Baker's Oldsmobile on the last lap to earn the victory. It seemed

Darrell Waltrip (88) and Yarborough battle in the Southern 500 at Darlington. After jockeying for the lead, the cocky young Waltrip crashed with Yarborough on lap 227 of 367. They rejoined the race and finished sixth and fifth, respectively. (T. Taylor Warren)

The new Oldsmobile Fastback made a strong debut at the 1978 Daytona 500, finishing second to Bobby Allison. Here Allison leads Yarborough with Buddy Baker (27), Dave Marcis (2), and Neil Bonnett (5) in close pursuit. Yarborough was the only other driver to finish on the lead lap with Allison. (Don Hunter)

Victory Lane in the Winston 500 in May was especially joyous because it was Yarborough's first victory since the Daytona 500. Yarborough took the checkered flag from Buddy Baker, when he made the pass on the last lap. (David Chobat)

Yarborough was nervous during qualifying for the Daytona 500 in his new Oldsmobile. "You wouldn't believe how unstable the car is," Yarborough said after this lap. Despite his complaints, he won the pole with a speed of 187.536 mph. (Don Hunter)

Left: The team hit its stride with the new Oldsmobile during the second half of the 1978 season, here pitting in the Southern 500 at Darlington. Yarborough rolled to victory, beating Waltrip by three seconds. (David Chobat)

Opposite: Junior and Yarborough show off their new Busch Beer paint scheme, which came with their Anheuser-Busch sponsorship. The car first ran at the 1979 Daytona 500. (Dozier Mobley)

the aerodynamically sound Oldsmobile was going to be the champ of the superspeedways.

By midseason, Yarborough had won just four times. But he went on to have an excellent second half of the year. He won six times and proved Oldsmobile's overall capability, as four of the victories came on short tracks.

At Ontario, California, the twenty-ninth race of the year, Yarborough crossed the line second to Allison. But it was more than enough to seal a third consecutive championship. Yarborough took it by 474 points over Allison.

The 1978 season had been Yarborough's best with Junior. He scored ten wins, twenty-three top-five finishes, and twenty-four among the top ten. His earnings of more than $623,505 were a NASCAR record. No other driver-team combination had been able to produce what Junior and Yarborough had, and it has never been matched in NASCAR history.

"I am very proud of the three championships," Yarborough says. "Being associated with Junior, who was one of the toughest drivers that ever lived and who was a good friend, well, that made winning my first championships as a driver and his first as a team owner that much better. It was great."

With 1979 came the Daytona 500 that is credited with being the catalyst that propelled NASCAR into the national limelight.

That February Junior's number 11 car debuted in Busch Beer racing colors, the result of a new sponsorship from Anheuser-Busch. Yarborough would drive Oldsmobiles primarily, but Junior would roll out a Chevrolet for his driver at selected races.

For the first time, the race would be telecast live, flag to flag. On the day of the race, February 18, a huge snowstorm blanketed much of the nation. People stayed home

and, to pass the time, millions of them decided to tune in CBS and see what stock car racing was all about. They got an eyeful.

On the thirty-second lap, Yarborough, Bobby Allison, and Bobby's younger brother, Donnie Allison, crashed along the backstretch. Then Donnie Allison lost a lap. Yarborough's Oldsmobile got stuck in the mud and lost three laps.

Timely caution flags enabled Donnie Allison and Yarborough to return to the lead lap. With 50 laps to go, they hooked up in the draft and pulled away from the field. It was obvious they would determine the outcome of the race. On the last lap, Donnie led going down the backstretch. Yarborough cut to his inside to make the classic "slingshot" pass. As his Oldsmobile moved under Donnie's, the younger Allison cut down and forced Yarborough toward the grass. The block did not intimidate Yarborough. He kept his foot on the gas and moved lower onto the track. Allison went with him, keeping the block in force. Yarborough found himself in the dirt, but he was not going to give in.

"Cale called me on the radio and said that Bobby had been waiting on him, was going to wreck him and all this stuff," Junior recalls. "I think Cale got caught up in a deal where he thought Bobby was going to keep him from catching Donnie. I told him to win the race regardless, go on and catch Donnie and do his job."

The next thing everyone saw was the two Oldsmobiles bouncing off each other. They split, then hit each other again. Then they locked together, heading in tandem toward the wall, which they hit in the third turn and spun into the infield. There, the cars came to a halt.

A.J. Foyt was in line to inherit the lead, but he backed off when he saw the caution lights flashing because of the Allison-Yarborough incident. Petty swept by with Waltrip

"And there's a fistfight in the third turn!" A national television audience watched Yarborough wind up for a swing at Donnie Allison, while Bobby Allison held desperately onto his feet and track officials attempted to separate the drivers. Yarborough, a former Golden Gloves boxer, swung his helmet first at Bobby, starting the infamous melee. (Daytona Racing Archives)

Yarborough leads the field early in the 1979 Daytona 500, the first race to be shown from start to finish on live network television. Yarborough would fall into second place behind Donnie Allison, battling him for the lead until the last lap, when they collided twice and came to a rest in the infield. (Daytona Racing Archives)

in tow. And it was Petty who took the victory, ending a forty-five-race skid. Everyone was thrilled with the finish, especially CBS. But it wasn't over.

"And there's a fistfight in the third turn!" CBS announcer Ken Squier said excitedly. The cameras caught only a portion of it. There was Donnie Allison, Yarborough and—Bobby Allison? Yarborough and the younger Allison, once they were out of their cars, were in no mood to share lunch. Bobby Allison simply cruised up to where the two stood in the third turn and stopped.

Yarborough was furious. He felt he had been set up by the Allisons and said so in strong language. Bobby dropped the window net on his car, and before he could get out, he took a shot from the helmet Yarborough swung at him.

Stunned, Allison said to himself that if he didn't address the situation immediately, he would have to run from Yarborough for the rest of his life. That started the melee. Bobby grabbed Yarborough by the throat. Yarborough kicked at Bobby. Donnie swung his helmet. It didn't last long, but it was enough.

What the good ol' boys of NASCAR had shown America was that they played in a rough-and-tumble sport, the likes of which most of the country had never seen.

CBS was delighted, and the ratings exceeded even its expectations.

Junior didn't care about ratings. He only knew that his driver had made up three lost laps and put himself in position to win the race, which he didn't.

"I knew Donnie had taken Cale right down to the grass," Junior recalls. "I knew what went on out there. And after it was over, somebody came running up to me in the garage after they wrecked and said they were over there fighting. I was asked if I intended to go over there and do something about it. I said, 'Hell no, let 'em kill each other as far as I'm concerned. The day is over for me.' "

"I couldn't believe that Bobby was over there after Donnie and I had wrecked," Yarborough says. "It was a situation where I lost my temper. We all did."

A few weeks later, when Yarborough was the subject of a roast, he joked, "You all know about what happened at Daytona, right? That wasn't a fair fight, two Allisons against me. I should have had one hand tied behind my back."

Yarborough remembers, "Everyone laughed. We just went right back to racing."

At first, NASCAR was indignant. It would not tolerate such behavior on the part of its competitors. A day after the race, it put the blame on Donnie Allison. He, like the others, was slapped with a $6,000 fine, but he was also given a severe probation. The Allisons fumed and demanded an appeal. Afterward, NASCAR amended its ruling. All three drivers were fined $6,000, but would be given back $1,000 per race over the next five races, provided they followed all NASCAR rules. The remaining $1,000 would be put into the point fund.

"I know some of the people who were making the judgment and their first reaction was the right reaction," Junior says. "That's what should have been done."

Junior has always suspected that a pro–Bobby Allison sentiment on the part of some of those passing judgment led to the reduced punishments.

"That doesn't make any difference," Junior says. "The facts speak for themselves. Donnie runs Cale plumb into the grass. Then Bobby stops out there and it ain't none of his business. He should have left Donnie and Cale over there and let them settle it between themselves. That is what should have happened. Both of 'em would have been fined and put on probation or something like that. But some people stick their noses in places where they ain't got no damn business."

Afterward, if NASCAR was outwardly displeased with what had happened, inwardly it knew the incident was the best thing that could have happened. It knew that the raucous finish to the race, helped in no small part by the legendary Petty's victory, had done more to propel NASCAR racing into the national consciousness than anything else the sanctioning body could have imagined.

The next race on the schedule was the Carolina 500 at North Carolina Motor Speedway. Ticket sales soared. And sure enough, Donnie and Yarborough got into it again, after just ten laps. Several drivers, among them Petty and Waltrip, were swept up in the multicar accident. This time the Daytona combatants were good boys. They called it a "racing accident." NASCAR took no action.

That didn't appease the others. Petty called the incident a "misjudgment in driving." Waltrip suggested someone needed to "drag Cale out of his car and whip his butt." Waltrip stopped short of offering to do it himself.

For Yarborough and Junior, the season was a shadow of what the previous three had been. Yarborough won just four times and finished fourth in the final Winston Cup point standings. The scrap for the championship was waged between Waltrip and Petty, which Petty won in the last race, at Ontario, by a mere eleven points.

The year 1980 was one of transition. New teams and new fans were streaming into NASCAR racing. The sport was taking root in the American consciousness. Corporate America—Anheuser-Busch, Quaker Oats, Citicorp, and others—was interested.

For Junior, it was business as usual. With Yarborough, he set out to win a fourth championship, but they were being seriously challenged by an upstart kid named Dale Earnhardt, who had won the Rookie of the Year title a season earlier.

In late summer of 1980, Cale Yarborough came to Junior and made a stunning revelation, confirming some gossip Johnson had heard.

Yarborough was headed to a team owned by M.C. Anderson, a wealthy developer from Savannah, Georgia. Anderson would permit Yarborough to cut back his schedule to eighteen races, down from thirty-one.

"In one way it surprised me a good bit, 'cause we were having a solid year and were in the thick of the points race for another championship," recalls Junior. "In another way it didn't surprise me, and I understood. Cale had two daughters at home, and he hadn't got to be around much as they were growing up. He was a fine family man, and he wanted to spend more time with those girls and his wife, Betty Jo. Cale decided he wanted to move to a team where he could run a limited schedule of just the major races."

It had to be an excruciating decision for Yarborough, who had risen to the top of the sport in Junior's cars. Even as he was developing plans to jump from Junior's team to Anderson's, the stocky South Carolina driver was in the process of scoring six victories, posting thirteen other top-five finishes and three other top tens, and winning fourteen poles and six other front-row starts while earn-

**"During those years, we had more fun than anybody," Junior says. "We had more fun losing races than most teams did winning them."**

ing a then career high of $567,890. And he was going to leave a team this strong?

"My daughters are at important times in their lives, and I want to be around more to share that with them," said Cale. "I want to be there for them."

The quest for the championship came down to the last race of the year, in Ontario. Going into the race, Earnhardt was atop the point standings by twenty-nine points over Yarborough. The situation was tense. Yarborough had made the chase close by winning the Atlanta Journal 500, a race in which Earnhardt had finished third. On November 15, they squared off at the 2.5-mile oval.

Waltrip, in his final season with DiGard, led most of the early laps but withdrew with engine failure after 145 of the race's 200 laps.

Yarborough was the leader at the time and led for most of the way until passed by Bobby Allison on lap 186. A flat tire seven laps later relegated Allison to the pits, and Benny Parsons, driving for Anderson, took over and earned the victory.

Yarborough finished third, and Earnhardt, after numerous miscues in the pits (he would say later his Rod Osterlund–owned team tried every way it could to give the championship to Yarborough), finished fifth. Earnhardt won the title by nineteen points.

The Junior-Yarborough association had come to an end.

"How would I rate those years with Junior?" Yarborough says. "You're asking me to blow my own horn. But they would have to run along the top. Yep, they would have to run along the top."

Yarborough had raced with Junior for eight glorious seasons that produced fifty-five wins and three consecutive Winston Cup championships.

Junior enjoyed how the South Carolinian emulated him as a driver.

"Either he or LeeRoy," Junior says in retrospect. "I have to count them as the drivers who were the closest to me. The difference was that Cale stayed with me a long, long time. That was something that hadn't happened to me earlier. I always knew if the right driver came along and he meshed with me and my cars, no one could top us eventually.

"During those years, we had more fun than anybody," Junior says. "We had more fun losing races than most teams did winning them."

Yarborough agrees. "We had a lot of fun," he says. "The atmosphere was good; Junior had good equipment and hard-working people. He was a dedicated racer, and doing it his way was good for us."

"It seemed that after Cale left, it all turned into business more than racing," Junior says. "Everything was dollars. See, racing had become so popular that big business moved in and started to dictate how you did things. They wanted the best results for their money. I could understand that, but I didn't want anyone else telling me what to do.

"You had to be in the sport when it wasn't money that motivated everyone to understand what I mean. When money started running the sport, it turned. You might say it's turned for the best, but for a lot of people, it turned for the worse."

**Junior speaks with long-time team member Henry Benfield in 1977. Benfield was the team's biggest practical joker during the Yarborough years. He put Ex-Lax into brownies, among other tricks. "I enjoyed working with Junior, he was a good man," Benfield says. "Junior never raised his voice to anyone and he would do anything for you. You don't find that today. Today, racing is a business, and it's not nearly as much fun." (NASCAR Winston Cup Scene Archives)**

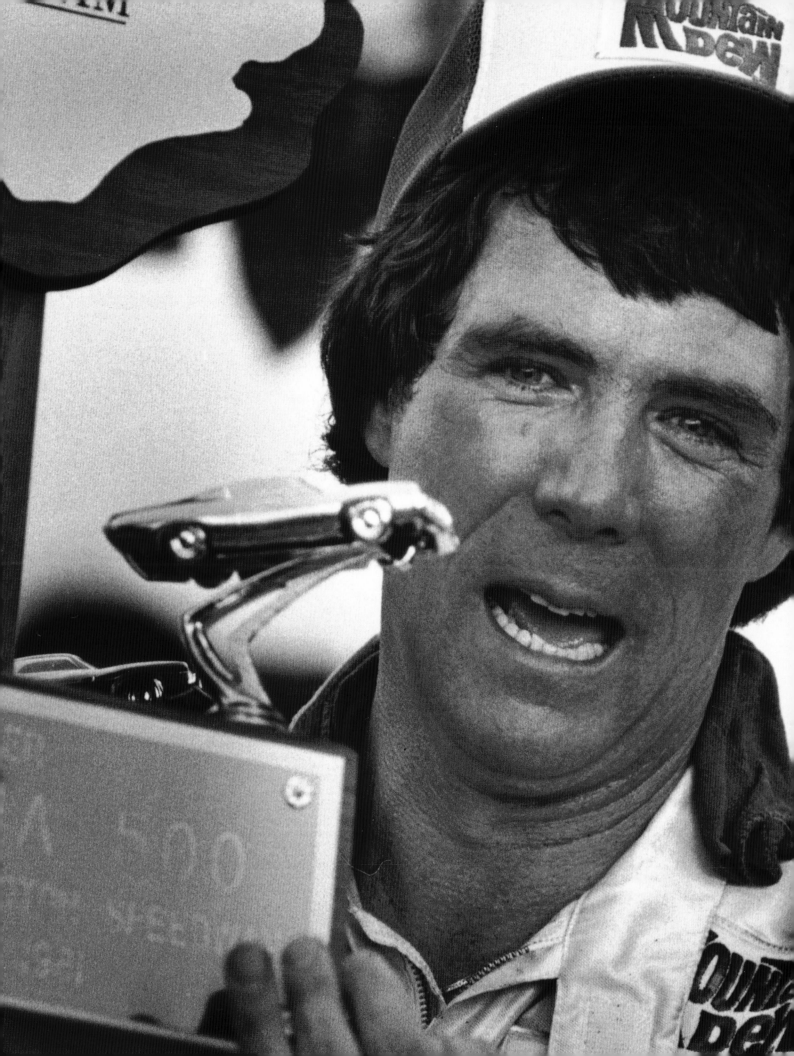

## CHAPTER THIRTEEN

It was a hot Friday before Labor Day at Darlington Raceway in 1979. Junior Johnson lay on his belly in the bed of a pickup truck in the garage area shade, watching as crewmen changed engines in the Johnson-owned Chevrolet that Cale Yarborough was to drive in the Southern 500.

Two reporters approached Junior, who appeared on the verge of dozing off. "Junior, we're hurting and we need your help," said one of the newsmen, sweating and red-eyed. "We partied almost all night, and both of us are hungover as hell. We're both in bad need of easy columns, something that won't take much thinking to write."

Junior laughed. "Everybody in NASCAR talks about your eye for judging driving talent," continued the reporter who was doing the talking for both. "We thought we'd file columns on who you foresee becoming the stars of the future."

Junior raised up on his elbows. "I don't think there's any doubt about it," said Junior. "I think it's going to be Ralph Earnhardt's boy and that mouthy little ol' boy over in Tennessee. What's his name? Waltrip? Yeah, that mouthy Waltrip."

# "That mouthy little ol' boy over in Tennessee."

Above right: **Junior fine-tunes the carburetor of the No. 11 Buick. After the win at Rockingham, several competitors questioned the size of the car's gas tank when Waltrip showed superior fuel mileage, running the last 108 laps without pitting. "I thought when Cale left Junior he would have taken that big gas tank with him," jabbed Bobby Allison. NASCAR ruled after the race that the gas tank was completely legal. (Don Hunter)**

Opposite: **Waltrip won at Rockingham in the Carolina 500, beating his predecessor, Cale Yarborough. "It didn't take long to see who got the best of the ride-swapping deals, did it?" said Waltrip. (Don Hunter)**

Junior poses with his hounds and the "Dew Crew" in front of the lineup of new Mountain Dew-sponsored cars for 1981. Kneeling from left to right are Henry Benfield, Junior, Eddie Thrap, and Jeff Wilson. The second row is J.V. Reins, Tim Brewer, Jeff Hammond, and Randy Call. In the back are Mike Hill, Harold Elliott, and Frank Justice. Darrell Waltrip, their new driver, is represented by the cut-out on the left. (Junior Johnson collection)

Junior was referring, of course, to Dale Earnhardt and Darrell Waltrip. "Why these two?" the newsmen asked. Junior grinned and his eyes sparkled mischievously. "Because they both have that one great quality it takes to make a great racecar driver."

"Which is?"

Junior was sitting up now, getting into the conversation. "They're both perfect assholes!" declared Junior, almost bellowing in laughter. The reporters chuckled nervously. "Uh, Junior," said one. "We can't get that in family newspapers. Could you couch it another way?" Junior laughed even harder and replied, "Yeah. They both think their crap don't stink!" The reporters chuckled at Junior's clever rephrasing, which he was well aware couldn't be printed in a family newspaper, either.

After teasing the newsmen a bit longer, Junior explained what he saw in the younger Earnhardt and Waltrip that made them such promising prospects: "I've seen that both of them are very determined to make it in racing, that they have a tough edge to 'em when it means gaining a position, and that both of 'em have worked on their own cars and hold a knowledge of what it takes to make a racecar run and handle."

Not even Junior could imagine at the time what a prophet he'd turn out to be. Nor what a pivotal role he would play in Waltrip's fulfilling his promise. Nor that he'd someday come very close to fielding cars for Earnhardt as well.

"When Darrell heard that Cale was leaving, he came by to see me at one of the races in the late summer of '80," says Junior. "Darrell wanted our ride. Darrell was under contract to the DiGard team, but him and the main owner, Bill Gardner, weren't getting along." Junior told Waltrip

he'd have to negotiate his way out of the contract, which had three years remaining. Gardner was reluctant to lose Waltrip, and understandably so. As a team since 1975 they had won twenty-six races and missed the 1979 championship by a scant eleven points, losing to Richard Petty in the season finale at Ontario. Negotiations were tough and, at times, very bitter as Bill Gardner and Darrell exchanged verbal barbs.

"I've developed an affliction," Waltrip joked at one race. "Every time I see Bill approaching it makes me want to hit somebody."

In late fall, an agreement was forged that would allow Waltrip to buy his way free of the DiGard contract. It was the first such deal in NASCAR. "Darrell and his lawyers came to Wilkes County, met me and my lawyers and we hammered things out to get together," says Junior, who'd observed in 1978 that he'd "like to have Darrell as a driver someday, but I doubt I could afford him." On December 22, 1980, Johnson and Waltrip finally made an appearance together to officially confirm their pairing.

The press conference was held at the relatively new Radisson Hotel on the square in downtown Charlotte. The deal was for a year, with options for the 1982 and '83 seasons. Mountain Dew, a soft drink, was going to be the team's sponsor. Ironically, "mountain dew" is a nickname for white liquor, like that Junior had hauled across the Carolinas, Tennessee, and Virginia.

Mountain Dew's colors were red, green and white. The paint scheme unveiled on the racecar at the press conference made it look something like a Christmas tree. A gaudy one. "It's appropriate the car is in Christmas colors, because this is the best present I ever had," proclaimed Waltrip. "I'm pumped up. All the ingredients are there for

Waltrip pulls away from his pit stall and loses his front left wheel during the 1981 Daytona 500. It was a rough start for the team after winning the Busch Clash and the second of the twin 125-mile qualifying races. Waltrip finished thirty-sixth in the 500. (Daytona Racing Archives)

Waltrip stretched his lead in the overall standings to 48 points after winning the Old Dominion 500 in Martinsville. Junior's former driver, Bobby Allison, was in close contention in second place after leading the points race by 341 in June. (T. Taylor Warren)

**"I've been in airplanes that were out of control that didn't scare me as bad," Waltrip said after a practice run.**

us to have one of the best teams that has ever been. I think we're going to set modern-era records for winning."

Junior agreed. "I think we're going to win a lot of races and championships. If we get some luck, we're going to be damn tough."

Speculation swirled about how much it had cost Waltrip to gain freedom from the DiGard contract. The figure mentioned most often was $320,000. "Let's put it this way: I'm startin' the season in a big hole financially, and I've got a long way to go to get even," said a grinning Waltrip, who never once disputed the talk of a buyout in the $300,000 range. "It wasn't near that much," Junior now concedes with a smile. "It was about half that. I know, 'cause I loaned Darrell the money." It was to prove a block-buster of a bargain, because "that mouthy little ol' boy from Tennessee" was about to show he had the talent to back up his talk, just as Junior had foreseen in 1973.

From the 1960s through 1981, NASCAR often opened its major tour at Riverside Raceway, a road course in mountainous, desert terrain east of Los Angeles.

It was here on January 9, 1981, that Darrell Waltrip took his first official laps in a car owned and fielded by Junior Johnson. The new combo made an auspicious start, as Waltrip won the pole for the Winston Western 500 at 114.711 MPH. There was an epidemic of optimism among team members that the new pairing would produce a victory right away. Waltrip led the first three laps on the 2.62-mile, eleven-turn layout, then slid off course. A bit later a fouled spark plug forced a long stay in the pits, and Waltrip wound up finishing seventeenth, a whopping eleven laps down to winner Bobby Allison.

A spectacular showing followed at Daytona International Speedway in the Busch Clash, a special event matching the previous season's pole winners. Downsized

cars had been mandated by NASCAR, and the teams were having trouble getting them set up properly. "I've been in airplanes that were out of control that didn't scare me as bad," Waltrip said after a practice run.

However, during the race Waltrip motored to the front on the ninth of the dash's twenty laps when Bobby Allison pitted because he thought a tire was going down. Waltrip was ahead the rest of the way. The victory was worth $71,500 to the Johnson outfit, it's biggest single purse to that point. Waltrip again qualified well in time trials for the Daytona 500, taking the outside front-row spot abreast of pole winner Bobby Allison. This put Waltrip on the pole for the second of twin 125-mile qualifying races leading to the 500. Despite his misgivings about the downsized cars, Darrell drove daringly during the 125. On the last lap, he dived almost to the apron in the fourth turn to pass Benny Parsons for the victory. Waltrip's moves drew ire from his rivals, including Richard Petty, who charged that Darrell had taken some "stupid" chances and "endangered other drivers' lives." "I was just trying to win," countered Darrell. Junior backed his driver.

The Johnson-Waltrip team's seemingly solid chance of sweeping the Clash, a 125-miler, and the 500 didn't ma-terialize. Waltrip never led a lap in the 500 and a blown engine on the 117th lap led to a finish of thirty-sixth. There were whispers that maybe the Johnson-Waltrip duo wouldn't be as dynamic as predicted. The next six races thoroughly dispelled this thinking. Waltrip won four of the races and was third in another.

The first Johnson-Waltrip regular season triumph came on February 22, 1981, in a 400-lap event at Richmond Fairgrounds Raceway. Waltrip, driving a Buick Regal, led 181 laps, including the final 46, to finish 3.6 seconds ahead of runner-up Ricky Rudd, Darrell's successor with the

Junior is ready with a fresh tire as Waltrip pits during the American 500 at Rockingham. Waltrip traded the lead five times with Bobby Allison over the last 43 laps before eventually winning by two car lengths. (Don Hunter)

At Charlotte Motor Speedway, Waltrip (11) and Harry Gant (33) lead the field, with Cale Yarborough (27) and Buddy Baker (1) in row two, during the opening lap of the National 500. Waltrip would go on to win while Gant, Yarborough, and Baker all had mechanical problems and did not finish the race. (Don Hunter)

DiGard team. "I hadn't doubted at any time that we were going to be a very strong team," says Junior. "And after what I saw at Richmond, I knew we were going to be stronger than even I had figured."

Darrell made it two in a row a week later in the Carolina 500 at Rockingham, this time winning a gas mileage gamble to beat his predecessor with the Johnson team, Cale Yarborough. "It didn't take long to see who got the best of the ride-swapping deals, did it?" crowed Waltrip. "I've already beat the guy who followed me and also the guy I followed."

Suspicious rivals pressed NASCAR officials to check the Waltrip-Johnson car's fuel cell because the fuel mileage was so decisive. It met regulations. "Not everyone was mollified, but we told them that was that," recalls NASCAR's Dick Beaty.

Waltrip next won the Valleydale 500 at Bristol in late March, bumping Earnhardt aside on the 118th lap en route to taking the lead. It was the first of frequent tangles the two were to experience while Darrell was driving for Junior. A week later Waltrip finished third in his first start for Junior at North Wilkesboro, and was almost apologetic afterward. "I'll get 'em next week," was his promise to Junior and the crew. He kept it, taking a rousing Rebel 500 after passing Harry Gant with eleven laps to go and then holding "Hurryin' Harry" off by a car length.

It was mid-April, and a lot of knowledgeable NASCAR observers had predicted Junior and Darrell would be "a-feudin', a-fussin', and a-fightin' " by now. Generally the reasoning was that Junior would become irritated by Darrell's brashness and cockiness. Plus, during Darrell's days with DiGard, he had said a lot of unkind things about Junior's team.

To wide surprise, the pairing produced a relative love-in.

"We've hit it off great," gushed Waltrip after the Darlington victory. "The rapport is really good, and I don't see it changing." Said Junior: "Yeah, there were some strong comments back and forth over the past few years. But you have that in racing. There never was any hatred, or anything approaching it. The goal on the part of both of us is the same—to win. When you want so bad to reach the same destination like that, it just naturally brings you together. Darrell is pretty much what I figured he'd be. Cale was good to work with. He liked to show up and simply drive the car. That was his way, and we made it work. On the other hand, Darrell wants to be involved more. He's interested in why things we do to the car work or don't. He offers input, and it's welcome. It's an added dimension for us."

"Where brickbats had been predicted, bouquets bloom in profusion," a *Charlotte Observer* columnist wrote of the two at the time.

Both Junior and Darrell predicted a "winning streak tear" for the team later in the season. They proved to be as proficient at prognostication as at racing. During the final fourteen races of the 1981 season, the Johnson-Waltrip team won seven times, was second five times, and was third

Left: Champagne flies in Victory Lane following Waltrip's $51,600 victory at Charlotte. Waltrip was ecstatic about the win, talking afterwards of his gamble to join Junior's team and buy out his old DiGard contract. "The money I won here about gets me even." Opening the bottle on the left is crew member Tim Brewer. (David Chobat)

Opposite: Playing an unfamiliar role as conservative team owner, Junior coached Waltrip from the pits to "save that car" during the season finale at Riverside. Waltrip's sixth-place finish secured the season championship, the first of his career. (David Chobat)

once. Four of the victories came consecutively in September and October at Martinsville, North Wilkesboro, Charlotte, and Rockingham.

Waltrip was ebullient after the Charlotte triumph. "The money I won here about gets me even," he said, referring to his buyout deal with DiGard. "At one time I was about dee-funct. Why, early this season, all I had to eat was hamburgers, and the crew guys were buying me those." Junior, listening, grinned and rolled his eyes as if to say, "Yeah, right."

"I'm so glad I had the guts to go ahead with the deal, which was completed in this time period a year ago," continued Waltrip. "A gambler wouldn't have taken the odds that it could be pulled off. But I went ahead because I remembered some advice my daddy gave me. He said, 'Boy, you can't worry about the mule going blind. You've just got to keep on loading the wagon.' "

The sensational autumn spree enabled Waltrip to rally back into the championship chase with Bobby Allison, who had led by a whopping 341 points in June. Waltrip had his Jaws persona working constantly during this period, goading Allison and his Ranier Racing team in a gusher of gamesmanship unprecedented in NASCAR.

Waltrip repeatedly commented that the pressure was on Allison, although Bobby remained atop the standings. "They're in big trouble," Waltrip said confidently after winning at Bristol on August 22. "We're just like a great football or baseball team that builds to a peak late in the season and wins it all."

"Why doesn't he just shut up and race?" groused one member of the Ranier outfit.

This was exactly the reaction Waltrip wanted. He increased the rhetoric, spicing what proved to be a dazzling duel over the final five races for the Winston Cup trophy.

Darrell finished second behind Neil Bonnett on September 20 at Dover, Delaware, in the CRC Chemicals 500. Allison was third. The outcome gave Waltrip a two-point lead. In Darrell's ensuing victories at North Wilkesboro, Charlotte, and Rockingham, the runner-up was Allison. Waltrip led by eighty-three points going into the season finale at Riverside. He took his eleventh pole of the year in time trials. Darrell led the first lap, gaining five bonus points immediately. Then, on strict orders from Junior, Waltrip feathered the throttle. As the race rolled on, Darrell became caught up in the action a few times and ran hard. Each time, Junior delivered a firm admonition via radio: "Back off, boy, and save that car." Allison won the race, but Waltrip finished sixth to take his first championship by fifty-three points. For perhaps the only time all season, Waltrip was momentarily speechless as he took a victory lap.

"I thought back to '79 and how much it hurt to lose by just eleven points to Richard [Petty]," said Darrell. "I thought of how much this meant to me and my wife, Stevie, and how much I owed to Junior. A rush went through my body."

"I knew from early in the season that we were going to gel really well by the second half of the year," Junior now reflects. "It took a little time for Darrell to get comfortable in our cars and to learn our way of doing things. The same for me and the crew boys to get used to him. We had good, solid cars. A really good crew. Dependable motors. It was just about an unbeatable combo."

The box score showed twelve victories, six second places, three thirds, and four other top tens. The winnings were $799,134, easily a single-season NASCAR record.

A couple of weeks after the season, Bobby Allison manfully made this concession: "Looking back, I think we

Left: According to Waltrip, Junior took great pride in achieving "firsts." One of them was being the first champion owner to be crowned at the prestigious Waldorf-Astoria in New York City after the 1981 season. At Junior's right during this press conference is Barney Hall of the Motor Racing Network. (Junior Johnson collection)

Opposite: Junior feeds his mule, Digger, on the farm in Wilkes County. Following the 1981 campaign, Junior gave Waltrip one his other prized mules, Rodie, as a congratulatory gift. "Every man needs a good mule," reasoned Junior. (NASCAR Winston Cup Scene Archives)

essentially let Darrell talk us out of the title. We had things going well, then we started paying more attention to what he was saying than we did to our own business."

During the same weekend the Johnson-Waltrip team was honored for the championship in New York, Darrell was named Driver of the Year for all forms of auto racing in America. Waltrip was honored during a luncheon at the elegant 21 in Manhattan.

Among those attending was Junior. A few years earlier when Yarborough had been named Driver of the Year, the Johnson–Yarborough party arrived at 21 and Junior was told he couldn't enter without a tie. The maitre d' offered to lend Junior a tie. Junior declined and instead had a hotdog from a sidewalk stand nearby for lunch.

Waltrip became emotional in accepting the Driver of the Year award. Darrell introduced his parents, Lee Roy and Margaret, and his in-laws, the Raders. There were stories that Frank Rader had opposed his daughter marrying a race driver. "Frank, I hope the award and this nice function today show I kept my promise," said Darrell, his voice cracking, "I promised if you'd give me a chance, I wouldn't mess up and let you down."

"You rotten kid," Rader said with obvious affection. It was a warm moment, especially for the Waltrip family, the Raders—and Junior.

The twelve victories scored by the Johnson-Waltrip team in 1981 was one victory short of Richard Petty's record for NASCAR's so-called modern era, dating to 1972. That's when the schedule was shortened to a more-manageable thirty-one races, down from forty-eight the year before.

"I figured we were going to be real, real strong again," says Junior. "The chemistry was as good as I've ever seen on a team. Darrell was loose and funny, and he didn't mind getting right in there with the crew boys and doing what had to be done."

What resembled a father-son relationship developed between Johnson and Darrell, sixteen years younger than Junior.

Delighted with the way things had worked out with Waltrip, Junior gratefully gave Darrell a prize mule named Rodie.

"Every man needs a good mule," reasoned Junior.

# CHAPTER FOURTEEN

For 1982, NASCAR revised the schedule so that the season opened in Daytona Beach rather than Riverside. Waltrip again drew angry words, this time from Neil Bonnett, for action he took during the last lap of a 125-mile qualifier en route to finishing second.

In the main event, Waltrip had the No. 11 Buick in the lead with forty-nine laps to go when he experienced Daytona 500 déjà vu. The engine failed again.

The outcome wasn't as bad as it might have been for the circuit's defending championship team. The 500 of 1982 was marked by incredible attrition, with only seventeen of the forty-two starters running at the finish. As a result, Waltrip finished twentieth. The race was won by Bobby Allison, who had taken over Waltrip's former ride with the DiGard team. That move was to forge a fierce rivalry with the Johnson contingent as the season rolled on.

Darrell and Junior got in gear spectacularly starting in March at Bristol, which was the third race. Their victory on the Tennessee track's high banks began a surge that produced five victories in an eight-race span. Wins followed at Atlanta, North Wilkesboro, Talladega, and Nashville.

## "Damn it, Junior, my name is Darrell!"

Above right: Junior watches Waltrip closely during the Coca-Cola 500 at Atlanta—and he saw Waltrip edge Richard Petty by "two inches" in the rain-shortened race. "It still ranks as the closest finish ever in Atlanta history and probably the closest anywhere," says Junior. (Don Hunter)

Opposite: Waltrip's visit to Victory Lane at the Valleydale 500 in Bristol started him on a tear in 1982. He went on to win four of the next seven races. (T. Taylor Warren)

Benny Parsons (28) and Waltrip (11) lead the field at the start of the Winston 500 in Talladega. Parsons won the pole, becoming the first-ever to qualify with a lap over 200 mph. Waltrip passed him on the last lap to take the checkered flag. (Don Hunter)

Waltrip experienced a temporary setback at the Southern 500 in Darlington when his engine blew on lap 240 of 367. Waltrip finished twenty-fourth and dropped 132 points behind Bobby Allison in the championship race. (David Chobat)

Junior breaks into an especially wide grin in recollection of the Atlanta and Talladega triumphs. "There was some great racing and two dandy finishes in those races," says Junior. "Darrell and Richard Petty were going to it at Atlanta, battling back and forth. It was threatening to rain, and finally big drops started falling. It was pretty apparent the race was going to be flagged to an end, and very shortly. Darrell was able to get under Richard in the final turn, and they came to the line side by side. NASCAR ruled that we won by two inches. It still ranks as the closest finish ever at Atlanta and probably the closest anywhere."

Waltrip made it a season sweep at Talladega after he won the Talladega 500 by one car length over Buddy Baker in August. It was the first time any driver had swept Talladega in the fourteen years that the second race had been run. (Don Hunter)

At Talladega, Junior slyly used some reverse psychology on Waltrip during the Winston 500. Junior sensed it might have been a slight factor in a pulse-pounding victory, and he occasionally used it again during the season. "Benny Parsons and Darrell were having a heck of a race," says Junior. "Benny was in a strong Pontiac, a car in which he'd become the first NASCAR driver to officially qualify at over 200 miles an hour [200.176 MPH]. It got down to the last three or four laps, and Benny was leading with Darrell second. I said into my radio, 'Pick it up a little bit down the backstretch, Cale.' I made like I had forgotten who my driver was. Darrell came back at me in a split second. 'Damn it, Junior, my name is Darrell!' he said, growling like a bear. I knew bein' called Cale would agitate him, and I knew he'd pick it up if there was anything left in the car."

There was something left, and Waltrip used it. Parsons maneuvered low to block Waltrip on the back straight the last time around the Talladega track. Waltrip promptly whipped to the upper groove and made the decisive pass, winning by three car lengths over Terry Labonte, who followed Darrell around Parsons.

Junior's cars were performing so well that publications that previously had printed little about auto racing were doing stories on his team. A writer from one such newspaper in the Carolinas was playing a "hard-hitting reporter" role while interviewing Junior. Sarcasm and skepticism tinged some questions and observations. "I'm sure that you go to engineers in Detroit to learn a lot about motors—right?" said the reporter.

"No," Junior responded coolly. "They come to me."

In late June the feud that had simmered between Waltrip and Yarborough since the "Jaws" incident at Darlington finally boiled over. It happened at Michigan

International Raceway in the Gabriel 400. After a long rain delay, Yarborough and Waltrip battled for the victory as darkness drew near. Yarborough held the lead as the final lap began. Darrell drew slightly ahead down the backstretch, then there was contact between the two cars in the third turn. Yarborough emerged ahead and stayed there to the flag stand.

After the checkered flag, Waltrip bumped Yarborough, then slid off the pavement into a muddy spot near the first turn. Darrell's car became mired, much to the mirth of Yarborough, who joked about how silly Waltrip looked stuck in the mud. Darrell expectedly jawed about the third-turn contact. This nettled Yarborough considerably. Cale observed that he probably was going to have to "meet Jaws in the Big K parking lot" to settle things. This, of course, never happened. Waltrip was way too smart to be lured into a tangle with the tough Yarborough, a former Golden Gloves champion.

As the season rolled to halfway, Allison took three of six races, including the Firecracker 400 at Daytona, which traditionally marked each tour's midpoint. The tussle for the title was a tight one between Allison and Waltrip. The duel developed into one of the most dramatic ever, with Waltrip and Allison essentially taking turns going to Victory Lane during the season's second half. It went like this immediately after the Firecracker 400: Waltrip won at Nashville; Allison won at Pocono; Waltrip won again at Talladega; Allison won at Michigan; and Waltrip won at Bristol. The Talladega triumph was especially significant in that Waltrip became the first repeat winner of the summer race in Alabama in fourteen runnings of the event.

Yarborough temporarily interrupted the Bobby-Darrell shootout by taking the Southern 500 at Darlington.

Allison scored at Richmond, and Waltrip, expectedly by now, won the next weekend at Dover. It was a heady time

to be a fan. And a team owner. "We were having a lot of fun," says Junior. "It was like two heavyweight fighters taking turns knocking each other down. I loved the intensity. To me, it was what racing is all about."

Waltrip then broke the pattern by making it two in a row with a victory at North Wilkesboro. After Harry Gant scored a popular win at Charlotte, Waltrip won two more in a row at Martinsville and Rockingham to equal the team's 1981 victory total and assume a lead of thirty-seven points. Allison won at Atlanta, while Darrell was third, placing the spread at twenty-two points in favor of Waltrip going into the season finale at Riverside.

Tension thickened among the Johnson and DiGard teams in the two weeks between the Atlanta and Riverside races. It was lump-in-the-throat tough as they arrived at the California road course. It seemed as if a writer from nearby Hollywood scripted the time trials. Waltrip won the pole at 114.995 mph, edging Allison, who took the second starting spot. Junior's facial expression never changed during the high drama of pole day. "There was a lot at stake, so it wasn't time for me to be showing a lot of emotion," says Junior. "I had to keep a calm head."

When qualifying was completed, Waltrip held an impromptu press conference outside in the sunny garage area. Bill Gardner walked by. "Nice lap," said Gardner. "Why, thank you," Waltrip replied very properly. Then, speaking just loud enough for the departing Gardner to hear, Waltrip added bitingly, "You're going to see 119 more just like it Sunday." (The Winston Western 500 covered 119 laps.) It didn't turn out quite that way.

Waltrip led laps one to four and then laps seventy-two through seventy-five. Allison led laps five through eight, seventeen through twenty and forty-six through forty-seven. Then Allison experienced two flat tires and stripped lug nuts that put him a lap back, a daunting disadvantage

Junior finally cracked a smile after
Waltrip placed third and Allison finished
sixteenth at Riverside, ensuring
Waltrip's second straight championship.
For Junior it was his fifth title in seven
years. (Junior Johnson collection)

# "Winning a NASCAR race is very satisfying, but I believe the most enjoyable thing I've known is having my dogs yapping and crawling all over me after they've treed a 'coon."

on a road course. With two laps to go the engine in Allison's car failed. Waltrip had problems, too, losing third gear when he missed a downshift around the lap fifty mark. Junior ordered an even more conservative pace than in 1981. Waltrip wound up third behind Tim Richmond and Ricky Rudd. Allison placed sixteenth. The outcome gave the Johnson-Waltrip operation the championship by a margin of seventy-two points.

It was the fifth title for Junior's team in seven years, an accomplishment that remains unmatched. The splendid final statistics: twelve victories, five more top-five finishes, three more top tens, seven poles, and a record $923,150 in purses.

Junior celebrated, in his way, by going raccoon hunting in the remote hollows and along the ridges where his family and friends once stoked their stills, making fine corn liquor. In these forests Junior unleashed his pack of hounds to chase 'coons.

"There's nothing like being way off in the mountains in the middle of the night," said Junior in the off-season between the 1982 and '83 NASCAR tours. "When the air is clear, the stars seem so close you could reach out and touch 'em. Nothing smells cleaner than the deep woods. It's about as far removed as you can imagine from the noise and smoke and crowds of speedways. I like to get out there, lean up against a tree, and take it all in. No matter what his problems, a man can really get at peace with the world when he gets out in the wilds like that.

"I've kept a pack of good 'coon hounds since I was a boy. I like racin' hounds against 'coons almost as much as I like racin' cars. Racin' dogs against an animal as smart as a 'coon is mighty enjoyable."

"When my schedule allows it, my hounds go huntin' five nights a week. My hounds paw off a lot of bark trying to get at 'coons they've treed."

Junior's pack at the time included four purebred Treeing Walkers, five Black and Tans, four Blue Ticks, and three Red Ticks.

The pack was well-known in raccoon hunting circles. Would-be buyers often approached Junior. "My hounds aren't for sale until they get eight or nine years old, when the best hunting times are over for them," he said. "Even then, if I'm fond of a dog, it's not for sale at any price. Why, I spent a fortune on one hound I was real attached to. It had a rare disease, something that was leading to deterioration of the jaw. My veterinarian brought in a specialist from one of the colleges in Georgia. They gave that hound all kinds of shots. They brought it around when other people were telling me to put the dog to sleep. Now it's one of the best hounds I've got.

"Winning a NASCAR race is very satisfying, but I believe the most enjoyable thing I've known is having my dogs yapping and crawling all over me after they've treed a 'coon. They're wanting to be petted and they're showing their love." Junior once was asked if he employed "electronic collars" in the training of his young hounds. He sneered in scorn. "I'd never mistreat a dog with one of them things," said Junior. "Electric collars ain't good for but one thing, and that's to wear out batteries."

Junior relaxed in the off-season with his 'coon hounds. "When my schedule allows it, my hounds go hunting five nights a week," said Junior. "My hounds paw off a lot of bark trying to get at 'coons they've treed." (Don Hunter)

# CHAPTER FIFTEEN

Stunningly, Junior took on a partner for the 1983 season.

In late autumn it was announced that Junior had sold half his racing operation to California businessman Warner Hodgdon, a former sponsor of Bud Moore's team.

It was another in a whirlwind string of deals negotiated by industrialist Hodgdon that had given him considerable clout in NASCAR. Hodgdon had bought a 50 percent interest in the speedways at Bristol, Nashville, North Wilkesboro, and Richmond. He was sponsor of both Winston Cup races at Rockingham. And he'd also purchased a half interest in the Rahmoc team, and named his friend Neil Bonnett as driver.

"Warner approached me either in late summer or early fall of '82 and asked about buying into my name, into Junior Johnson and Associates," says Junior. "He offered a deal that would benefit the company. It happened during one of those periods that back then often came about in NASCAR when almost everybody was scrapping for sponsors." Hodgdon joined Junior just in time to share a season marked by trouble and turmoil.

## "Junior is up to his old tricks."

Above right: Junior and new partner, Warner Hodgdon, discuss business strategy in Junior's office. Hodgdon had been a former sponsor of Bud Moore's team. (Dozier Mobley)

Opposite: Junior speaks with crew members in the team shop at Ingles Hollow. The competition between Waltrip and Bonnett became so intense Junior had to separate the team shops following 1984. (Don Hunter)

Left: The No. 11 Chevrolet sported a new Pepsi paint scheme in 1983. Pictured behind the car are, from left to right, crew members J.V. Reins, Jeff Hammond, Doug Richert, Mike Hill, and Henry Benfield. (David Chobat)

Below: Waltrip and Junior talk at North Wilkesboro before his first win of the 1983 season in the Northwestern Bank 400. Waltrip led 245 of the 400 laps, beating Bobby Allison. (David Chobat)

The trouble came almost immediately. During the season-opening Daytona 500, Waltrip became entangled in an accident that resulted from Earnhardt's blown engine. Waltrip slammed into the inner wall off the fourth turn exceedingly hard and was knocked unconscious.

At nearby Halifax Hospital, doctors determined that Waltrip had suffered a concussion. He was held overnight and released. Prematurely, it turned out.

At Richmond the next weekend, Waltrip gamely rejoined the team. He seemed subdued and there were no flashes of his feisty nature. Waltrip qualified fourth, but a mechanical problem developed in the 400 and he dropped out less than halfway into the race.

"Darrell was hurt way worse than any of us suspected," says Junior. "We should have seen it then, but for some reason we didn't. Darrell was in a fog. Some time afterward, Darrell admitted to me that he didn't remember a thing about the Richmond race. He didn't hardly remember going there.

"It didn't show for a long time, but I think that wreck at Daytona kept Darrell in future years from accomplishing a lot he might have done if it hadn't happened. It had a far-reaching affect."

Waltrip doesn't feel nearly so strongly about the long-term effects, essentially dismissing the idea. However, he concedes that pressing on at Richmond shortly after being knocked out probably was a foolish thing to do. "Hindsight makes you a lot smarter," says Waltrip.

Waltrip snapped back to finish a solid third in mid-March at Rockingham. In mid-April he made Junior and the Wilkes County home folks happy, scoring his first victory of 1983 at North Wilkesboro to start another sizzling streak. Darrell won four of six, adding victories at Martinsville, Nashville, and Bristol during the next five weeks.

The rivalry between the Allison-DiGard team and the outfit led by Junior burst into flames again.

The DiGard camp insinuated that the Johnson team was breaking the rules. This was based, according to Allison, on information passed along by a former employee who had left the Johnson-Hodgdon team. Allison indicated after winning at Dover that his team had implemented the "tricks" of Johnson. Allison smilingly, tauntingly refused to divulge specifics.

Waltrip won the next week at Bristol and hardly could wait to get to the victor's interview to deliver a zinger at Allison.

"Obviously, we haven't given away all our secrets," said Waltrip, much to Junior's delight.

A winless three months followed for Waltrip and the Johnson-Hodgdon team. Allison helped extend it in late July at Talladega as Waltrip and Earnhardt battled for victory. Allison, lapped, gave Earnhardt a drafting boost from behind on the last lap to edge Waltrip.

At the 1983 Daytona 500, Waltrip suffered a severe concussion when he slammed into the inner wall coming out of the fourth turn and was knocked unconscious. "I think that wreck at Daytona kept Darrell in future years from accomplishing a lot he might have done if it hadn't happened. It had a far-reaching effect," says Junior. (Daytona Racing Archives)

Above: At Charlotte during the Miller 500, Waltrip pitted out of gas and stalled. To restart the car, the crew pushed it out of the pits, gaining enough speed for the engine to turn over. The race was one of the most controversial in NASCAR history when the victorious Richard Petty was found to have an oversized engine. Despite the infraction, NASCAR let Petty keep the victory and Waltrip remained second. (NASCAR Winston Cup Scene Archives)

Left: Waltrip leads Allison during the 1983 season when both drivers were jockeying for the points lead. Allison was driving for Waltrip's former team, DiGard. He maintained a commanding lead throughout the year and held off both Waltrip's car and his mouth to win the championship by 47 points. (Daytona Racing Archives)

Waltrip and Junior at North Wilkesboro before his first win of the season in the Northwestern Bank 400. Waltrip led 245 of the 400 laps, beating Bobby Allison. (David Chobat)

"Bobby shouldn't have been sticking his nose into it," an irritated Junior said after the race. "He should have let Dale and Darrell go one on one."

The nonwinning streak ended at Bristol in late August. Waltrip's driving and Junior's knowledge of the engine combinations and chassis setup needed at the track were simply too great for others to overcome. The win vaulted Waltrip into second place in the points race, forty-one down to Allison.

Darrell oiled his jaws.

"We're only forty-one down? I'd say we've got them right where we want 'em," needled Waltrip.

This time, though, neither Allison nor his teammates were listening. Allison mounted a tear of his own to win three in a row. He started the streak by taking Darlington's Southern 500, then scored at Richmond and Dover to lead by 101 points. Allison and Waltrip next finished second and third behind Ricky Rudd at Martinsville. Waltrip, predictably, scored again in the Junior-prepared car at North Wilkesboro to trail by ninety-one.

The following October weekend at Charlotte produced one of the most controversial incidents in NASCAR history. On the 295th of the 334 laps at the Charlotte track, Darrell finally worked into the lead for the first time. He remained there until the 312th lap, when Richard Petty appeared, seemingly from nowhere. Petty's car looked like a blue blur as he passed Waltrip in the second turn. Petty, who also hadn't led previously, charged to the checkered flag by the runaway margin of 3.1 seconds.

"I knew right away that something wasn't right," says Junior. "I think I said at the time that Richard went by our car like it was tied. I can still see it in my mind and that's exactly how it looked. I felt I knew what Richard's team had done to beat us. They had put softer compound left-side tires on the right side of the car during the last pit stop. This gave Richard much better traction in the turns and made him faster. I sent two of my boys to Victory Lane to take a look at Richard's tires. They came back and confirmed what I'd guessed.

"NASCAR officials already had noticed the violation, and they ordered the car taken to a secure area, a stall in the Unocal building, for a complete inspection. Before they could get started looking at the engine, Maurice Petty, Richard's brother walked in and told them they needn't bother tearing it down. He confessed the engine was too big."

NASCAR checked anyway. The engine measured 381.983 cubic inches. The maximum allowed was 358. Maurice Petty and the crewmen absolved Richard of any complicity in the violations. Waltrip, understandably, was wailing about being wronged. Junior, tired of waiting as NASCAR officials huddled about what to do, went home to Ingles Hollow.

Just before midnight the decision was made. Petty would keep the victory, but he was fined $35,000 and docked 104 points. "I should be the winner of the race," insisted Darrell. Junior scorched NASCAR when reached by phone at home. "Here it is, fifteen years later, and it still burns me," says Junior. "I don't have any problem with Richard. I have nothing against him in the thing. My fuss is what NASCAR did. Two weeks before, NASCAR had taken four laps away from Tim Richmond for using illegal tires at Martinsville. Four laps! NASCAR said the difference was that at Charlotte, they took Richard's money. I told them, 'Like hell it was Richard's money! By all rights it was my money!'"

The incident proved extremely embarrassing for NASCAR and its biggest, best-liked star. Some fans maintained a

wakelike vigil for a couple of days at the Petty Enterprises compound at little Level Cross, North Carolina. Said one, clinging to the fence, "It's almost like God has sinned."

The runner-up finish at Charlotte left Waltrip, trying to match Cale's run to three straight titles with Junior, trailing Allison by sixty-seven points. Waltrip cut the deficit to twenty-seven at Rockingham but fell sixty-four back at Atlanta. "We've still got a fair shot," said Junior, looking to the last race at Riverside. The team's hopes were heightened when Waltrip won the pole. Allison qualified sixth. Allison cut a tire in the early going, and the suspense increased.

Allison was able to remain on the lead lap, although Waltrip and others were setting a torrid pace up front. This time it was Allison running conservatively to preserve points. On the 111th of the race's 119 laps, Waltrip and Tim Richmond tangled coming out of a hairpin-type final turn and spun to the infield. Both were able to continue, but Waltrip wasn't far ahead of Allison. Darrell placed sixth; Allison was ninth. After years of trying, Bobby Allison finally had a championship, by a margin of forty-seven points, over Waltrip, who finished with six wins, sixteen other top-five finishes, three other top tens, and $865,184 in winnings.

The Riverside race was won by drawling young Georgian Bill Elliott, who scored his first victory at the Winston Cup level.

For the second straight late autumn, Junior had a startling announcement in November of 1983. Amid much fanfare during Atlanta's race week, the Johnson-Hodgdon team announced it would switch from Pepsi sponsorship to the backing of Anheuser-Busch in 1984. Also, there was to be a two-car operation, and both would display similar Budweiser paint schemes. Hodgdon was bringing his

friend Bonnett over from the Rahmoc team to drive machinery prepared by Johnson's veteran crew.

"Darrell didn't like the idea of a two-car deal a bit," says Junior. "Except for Carl Kiekhaefer's operation in the early '50s, no one had made it work. I told Darrell I'd make sure he wasn't held back any by Neil's team, and I kept my word."

Bonnett was scintillating in his debut in Junior's car, charging to the front on the last lap of the Busch Clash at Daytona to upset Buddy Baker, who'd led the first nineteen laps. Waltrip finished sixth. Another deep disappointment awaited Waltrip in the Daytona 500. He drove masterfully, saving his car until the final fourth of the race. Waltrip took the lead on the 162nd lap and stayed there through the 199th. Then archrival Yarborough came slingshotting by, bringing Earnhardt with him. Darrell finished third. The Junior-Darrell combination clicked again at Bristol on April 1. It was Junior's eighth straight win on the Tennessee track. "The way we had that place figured out at the time, it would have been a big, big April Fool's joke if anybody else had won," says Junior. Darrell next won the TranSouth 500 at Darlington, a race marred by so many wrecks that Waltrip was led to comment, "It was like putting a bunch of piranha in a pool with one piece of meat."

On May 12 at Nashville an incident occurred that caused a rift within the Waltrip and Bonnett team. Darrell was the leader starting the 418th of 420 laps when the yellow and white flags showed simultaneously. The caution was forced by an accident. Bonnett whipped by his nominal teammate, and NASCAR officials gave Bonnett the checkered flag. Waltrip protested that he had been passed illegally. Two days later, NASCAR agreed that a rule had been "misinterpreted" and Waltrip was declared the winner, with Bonnett second.

On August 12, Waltrip took Junior's No. 11 Chevy to Victory Lane a fourth time, using fuel mileage to beat Elliott at Michigan. Junior cannily figured out a carburetor setting that enabled Waltrip to make one less pit stop for fuel than most of the team's top rivals. The team had another of its usual strong autumn runs, taking three of five by winning at Richmond, Martinsville, and North Wilkesboro.

Waltrip scored seven victories in 1984, one more than during the previous season. He added six other top-five finishes, seven other top tens, four poles, and $731,023. Even so, despite winning just two races, Labonte was a runaway leader in the points race for the title.

"Winning ought to award more points—bonus points," complained Waltrip. "We've won more than anybody, and we should at least be in contention for the championship. We ought to have a system that rewards running to win, not running just to finish."

Bonnett, meanwhile, was winless. He was a runner-up twice, had two other top-five finishes, seven other top tens, four poles, and $282,533 in earnings.

Major changes were fast approaching for Junior, Darrell, and Bonnett.

Hodgdon had fallen into deep financial trouble, the victim of an unfaithful employee in California. A bid-rigging scandal had evolved, and Hodgdon faced lawsuits totaling $53 million, which forced him to file for bankruptcy. Hodgdon lost ownership of the speedways he was involved in. In mid-January of 1985, Junior filed foreclosure papers because Hodgdon owed a considerable amount of money.

Bonnett (12) leads Harry Gant (33) en route to victory in the 1985 Carolina 500 at Rockingham. Despite Hodgdon's departure from the ownership group during the off-season, Bonnett remained with the team for two more years. (Don Hunter)

Hodgdon's part of the racing team was auctioned off on the courthouse steps by the Wilkes County clerk of court. There was one bidder on a bitterly cold, icy morning: Junior Johnson.

For the sum of approximately $200,000, Junior had full control of his team again.

"Warner's intentions were very honest," says Junior. "He helped my whole organization at that time. I welcomed the whole deal he brought to us. He played a key role in me getting back with Anheuser-Busch with two cars. I think he helped the tracks he was involved with, too. I'm sorry for what happened to him."

Despite Hodgdon's departure, Bonnett remained a part of Junior's operation for both the 1985 and 1986 seasons as Waltrip's teammate. Eventually, the competition became so great between the two teams at Ingles Hollow that Junior based them in different shops separated by a small creek. At times the chasm between the sniping teams was so wide, that creek might as well have been the Grand Canyon.

The 1985 season was one of the most memorable in NASCAR history, and the Junior-Waltrip team played a starring role. During the off-season, officials of series-sponsoring R.J. Reynolds Tobacco Company announced the creation of two rich special programs—the Winston all-star race, which was to be an annual event, and the Winston Million Bonus. The latter, a $1 million prize, would go to a driver winning three of the Big Four races in a season.

Waltrip got off to a solid start in 1985. He was runner-up in both the Busch Clash and a Daytona 125-mile qualifier, then took third place in the Daytona 500. Bonnett won for the first time for Junior in the Carolina 500 at Rockingham on March 3, passing Harry Gant in a metal-swapping battle for the lead in the final turn on the last lap.

"I think the world of Harry," says Junior, recalling the race. "But it sure tickled me to see one of my drivers win like that. It was great racing, a throwback to NASCAR's early days."

On April 21, Bonnett scored again, helping provide Junior with one of his proudest moments ever at home at North Wilkesboro. The runner-up in a "double dip" for the Johnson operation was Waltrip, who finished second by a car length.

In the meantime, Elliott was overwhelming his opposition on superspeedways. The Ford-driving Georgian won five big track races through early May. Included were the Daytona and Winston 500s, victories that put him in position to collect the Winston Million in the Coca-Cola 600 at Charlotte.

Charlotte Motor Speedway owner Bruton Smith and general manager Humpy Wheeler had successfully lobbied RJR for the inaugural running of the Winston all-star show, a race matching the circuit's winners from the year before. The special event, covering 105 miles, was held May 25 with a field of twelve. After all drivers made a mandatory pit stop between laps thirty and forty of the 70-lap race, Gant led Terry Labonte by 2.7 seconds, with Waltrip almost another second behind in third place. Starting the final ten laps, Gant looked a sure winner, leading Waltrip, now in second place, by 3.1 seconds. Waltrip then began gaining significantly each time around the 1.5-mile track. On lap sixty-nine, Waltrip whipped into the lead and then opened that lead to ten car lengths.

As Waltrip took the checkered flag for a $200,000 prize, the engine in his Chevy erupted in a puff of smoke. Gant's car owner, Johnny Hayes, erupted, too. Hayes angrily charged that Waltrip had detonated the engine intentionally so that it couldn't be inspected by NASCAR. "Junior is up to his old tricks," said a seething Hayes. Gant was hot as well.

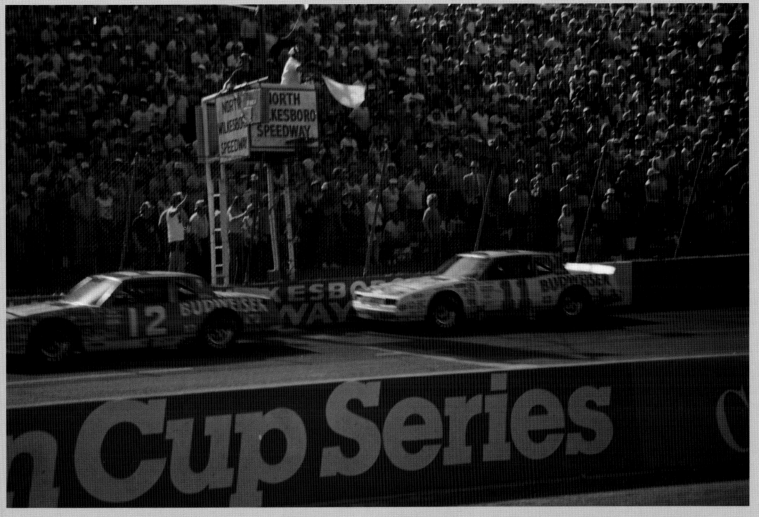

Bonnett (12) held off his teammate in the Northwestern Bank 400 to give Junior's team a triumphant one-two finish on his hometown North Wilkesboro track. It was Bonnett's fifteenth career victory. (T. Taylor Warren)

Bonnett's crew chief Doug Richert (left) celebrates with Junior and Bonnett in Victory Lane after the Northwestern Bank 400. Richert got a prominent start in NASCAR after holding the crew chief position with Dale Earnhardt's championship team in 1980. He was 20 years old at the time. (T. Taylor Warren)

Cale Yarborough (28), Waltrip (11), and Bonnett (12) race in the Southern 500 at Darlington. Yarborough finished a solid second, but no one could catch young Bill Elliott, who won the race and the Winston Million bonus. Waltrip finished seventeenth, Bonnett fourth. (T. Taylor Warren)

"I agree it looked suspicious," says Junior in retrospect. "They figured I'd ordered Darrell to clutch the thing to blow the motor to pieces. Basically, it was a freak thing. I'd told my engine boys to build a motor that would perform at the maximum for a little over a hundred miles, and that's what they did. They figured it to the foot, it turned out. The engine was tore up, yeah, but not so much it couldn't be inspected. NASCAR did check it after the race. They checked the bore and stroke, and it was legal."

Waltrip made it a Charlotte sweep a day later, on May 26, in the Coca-Cola World 600. Elliott, under immense pressure worsened by a wild media frenzy, won the pole for the 600 but didn't run well in the 400-lap race. As the 600 neared conclusion, it was again a Waltrip-Gant showdown. Gant led from the 328th lap to the 390th, when he had to pit for fuel. Waltrip remained on the track.

"Darrell's wife, Stevie, was sitting in our pit, keepin' track of the laps and figuring gas mileage," says Junior. "She became very concerned. She told me we weren't going to make it on fuel, that we were going to be about three or four laps short. I'd already decided that I was going to leave Darrell out there. If he ran out of fuel, it was going to be with us trying to win the race. Darrell made it, just as I thought he would. But he ran out of gas on the cooldown lap. We cut it close again and won. Our secret in that deal was making sure we got all the fuel out of the tank, or fuel cell. We set the tank up at an angle where the last bit of gas would get hemmed up when the car was on the banking. The gas then would go into the fuel line. Also, I was doing some carburetor work in this period and had developed a few little touches. We were running the carburetors real lean, but still not burning the motors up."

Elliott, out of the Charlotte cauldron, took four of the next seven races en route to a final shot at the $1 million in the Southern 500 at Darlington. Waltrip and Bonnett were winless in the span. Elliott dramatically edged Yarborough to pocket the Winston Million. In the process, Elliott forged a commanding 206-point lead over Waltrip in the run for the championship, with only eight races remaining. It appeared Elliott couldn't be overtaken. Waltrip was undaunted. He was about to put his sharp-tongued gamesmanship in high gear.

"It ain't no fun needling the Elliott boys—Bill and his brothers, Ernie and Dan," said a puckish Waltrip. "They won't talk back to you. They just stand and look at you."

Coincidentally or not, the bottom fell out for "Million Dollar" Bill and his team. Waltrip won the next weekend at Richmond to trail by 153 points; he was second to Gant at Dover to pull within 86; then second to Earnhardt at Martinsville to cut the margin to 23. Elliott was enduring an epidemic of mechanical failures—and of Waltrip's mouth and actions. Waltrip, grinning in mischievous glee, used his right hand at opportune moments to mimic the Pac-Man computer character chewing away.

"That Pac-Man stuff would have gotten to about anybody," says Junior. "It wouldn't have surprised me if some of the Elliott people had busted Darrell one."

At North Wilkesboro on September 29, Waltrip finished fourteenth to the luckless, harried Elliott's thirtieth. That outcome put Waltrip in the lead for the title by fifty-three points. Elliott regained form to finish second to Yarborough at Charlotte, but Waltrip was fourth, to lose only ten points. Waltrip next scored his third victory of the year by taking the Nationwise 500 at Rockingham and gained fifteen as Elliott was fourth. Elliott triumphed on his Atlanta home track and got the fifteen points back as Waltrip finished third.

Waltrip held a twenty-point lead going into the Riverside season finale. Were Waltrip's old complaints about the point system haunting him? He led the standings despite winning

only three times, while Elliott, who had scored a modern-era record eleven victories on superspeedways, was in second place. "No, I still think it's unfair," Waltrip said.

A torrid shoot-out was anticipated at Riverside. An anticlimactic season ending developed instead. An inexpensive bolt sheared off Elliott's transmission on the sixth lap, forcing a long stay in the pits. Junior reacted by again ordering Waltrip into a conservative pace. Waltrip finished seventh to Elliott's thirty-first. Junior and Darrell captured their third title together. It was the sixth for Junior in ten years.

The scoring difference in favor of Junior and Darrell was fifteen top-five finishes in addition to the three victories. Elliott had just five top fives aside from his wins. Bonnett enhanced the showing of Junior's operation by placing fourth in the point standings. The two Johnson teams combined for five victories, twenty-nine top-five finishes, thirty-nine top tens, and $1,848,518 in winnings. "We'd like to have won more, but looking back, we had good, solid seasons with both teams, considering that the circuit was getting real, real competitive," says Junior. "I was enjoying myself."

**Above:** Waltrip leads eventual winner, Ricky Rudd (15), in the season finale at Riverside. Waltrip finished seventh, but Elliott's disastrous thirty-first place finish sealed the championship for Jaws. (Don Hunter)

**Below:** Waltrip accepts the championship trophy at Riverside. It was the third title he had earned driving a car for Junior and the sixth title in ten years for a Junior-owned team. (Don Hunter)

# CHAPTER SIXTEEN

For Junior Johnson, a man of the mountains, 1986 was a year of peaks and valleys. Also of controversy and a case of seeming contradiction.

The highest peak was a lofty one, indeed. The story broke on January 12, the eve of the National Motorsports Press Association's annual convention in Charlotte. Junior had just learned that a long-standing wish had come true: He had been granted a presidential pardon for his moonshining conviction in 1956. President Ronald Reagan had signed the papers on December 26, 1985.

"There's no way I ever could have received a better Christmas present," Junior said upon being told of President Reagan's action. "I filed the request for a pardon about five years ago, in 1981. I never gave up hope that it would come through. I was told when I filed that it probably would take quite some time."

The pardon was full and unconditional, retroactive to the completion of his sentence. A presidential pardon is a sign of forgiveness. It does not erase or expunge the record of conviction and does not indicate innocence. It does generally restore basic civil rights, which are lost upon conviction of a felony. Among these are the right to vote.

# "Dale stepped over that line."

Above right: **Junior met Reagan in the Oval Office for the official presentation of his presidential pardon. Junior says Reagan "made a strong impression" and that he was "a very nice person, warm and friendly. He wasn't very knowledgeable about racing, and didn't try to make like he was." (Junior Johnson collection)**

Opposite: **Despite his success with Junior, Waltrip (back to camera) decided to leave the team before 1987 and join Rick Hendrick. Junior thought Waltrip left with the impression he could convince Budweiser to follow him with their sponsorship. But Waltrip was unaware that Junior and Hodgdon had already negotiated an extension with the sponsor through at least 1989. (Don Hunter)**

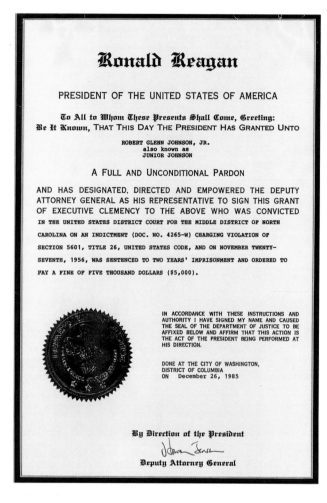

# Ronald Reagan

## PRESIDENT OF THE UNITED STATES OF AMERICA

To All to Whom These Presents Shall Come, Greeting:
Be It Known, THAT THIS DAY THE PRESIDENT HAS GRANTED UNTO

ROBERT GLENN JOHNSON, JR.
also known as
JUNIOR JOHNSON

### A FULL AND UNCONDITIONAL PARDON

AND HAS DESIGNATED, DIRECTED AND EMPOWERED THE DEPUTY ATTORNEY GENERAL AS HIS REPRESENTATIVE TO SIGN THIS GRANT OF EXECUTIVE CLEMENCY TO THE ABOVE WHO WAS CONVICTED IN THE UNITED STATES DISTRICT COURT FOR THE MIDDLE DISTRICT OF NORTH CAROLINA ON AN INDICTMENT (DOC. NO. 4265-W) CHARGING VIOLATION OF SECTION 5601, TITLE 26, UNITED STATES CODE, AND ON NOVEMBER TWENTY-SEVENTH, 1956, WAS SENTENCED TO TWO YEARS' IMPRISONMENT AND ORDERED TO PAY A FINE OF FIVE THOUSAND DOLLARS ($5,000).

IN ACCORDANCE WITH THESE INSTRUCTIONS AND AUTHORITY I HAVE SIGNED MY NAME AND CAUSED THE SEAL OF THE DEPARTMENT OF JUSTICE TO BE AFFIXED BELOW AND AFFIRM THAT THIS ACTION IS THE ACT OF THE PRESIDENT BEING PERFORMED AT HIS DIRECTION.

DONE AT THE CITY OF WASHINGTON, DISTRICT OF COLUMBIA
ON     December 26, 1985

By Direction of the President

Deputy Attorney General

**Left:** President Ronald Reagan signed an official presidential pardon for Junior on December 26, 1985. Reagan was not a racing fan, but was familiar with the popularity of the sport and the success of NASCAR. In 1984 he had attended Richard Petty's 200th victory at Daytona. (Junior Johnson collection)

**Opposite:** At Richmond, Junior scowls on pit road after Dale Earnhardt spun out Waltrip on lap 398 of the 1986 Miller 400. With Waltrip and Earnhardt off the pace, Kyle Petty charged to the front and led the last two laps for the checkered flag. (David Chobat)

Junior and good friend, R.J. Reynolds representative Ralph Seagraves, share a laugh at North Wilkesboro. Officials at R.J. Reynolds, including Seagraves, and NASCAR's France family, among others, spoke to President Reagan on Junior's behalf about the pardon. (David Chobat)

Because of his felony, Junior's induction into the North Carolina Sports Hall of Fame was held up until 1982. He had been nominated practically every year since becoming eligible in 1971, but the chairman of the induction committee, crusty *Raleigh News and Observer* sports editor Dick Herbert, arbitrarily refused to count votes for Junior, growling that "Johnson is a common criminal."

"I didn't think it was possible to be any happier than gettin' into the North Carolina Hall of Fame," said Junior. "But the pardon tops that. A lot of people helped with this pardon, and I sure want to thank them." Among those approaching Reagan on Junior's behalf were NASCAR's France family and top officials of R.J. Reynolds Tobacco.

Buoyed by the pardon, Junior hoped for strong 1986 showings by Waltrip and Bonnett as a further boost. This didn't develop. Waltrip finished third in the Daytona 500 for the third year in a row. Bonnett experienced a broken wheel on the 100th lap, hit the wall and swept Joe Ruttman, Buddy Baker, Harry Gant, and Yarborough into the crash.

Waltrip and Earnhardt were dominant the following Sunday at Richmond in the Miller 400 and raced headlong into a raging ruckus, the most controversial since Yarborough tangled with Donnie Allison at Daytona in 1979. Earnhardt was the leader starting the 398th of 400

# "I'm getting off an ol' mule and onto a good, strong thoroughbred," says Waltrip. Retorted Junior, "I've had a jackass driving my car, and now I'm rid of him."

laps at Richmond Fairgrounds Raceway, a .542-mile oval. Waltrip was on his bumper. Waltrip whipped to the inside and pulled ahead down the backstretch. But going into the third turn, the left front of Earnhardt's car and the right rear of Waltrip's made contact. Both drivers spun and crashed hard into the steel rails. Ruttman, running third, also wrecked. Kyle Petty cleared the melee and came back around to take the white and yellow flags. The next lap, Kyle took the checkers, becoming the first third-generation winner in Winston Cup history.

Anger flared on pit road between the Johnson-Waltrip and Earnhardt-Richard Childress teams. "It wouldn't have been much worse if Earnhardt had took a cocked pistol and put it to Darrell's head," declared a fuming Junior. "Dale just clipped him and threw him into the wall."

Retorted Earnhardt: "If I had been trying to wreck him, I sure as hell wouldn't have wrecked myself. I was simply trying to dive back underneath him and get back to the front, and I didn't make it."

NASCAR acted swiftly. The next day Earnhardt was fined $5,000 for reckless driving. Additionally, he was put under a $10,000 bond and placed on probation for the rest of the year. "There is a fine line between hard racing and reckless driving," said NASCAR competition director Bill Gazaway. "Dale stepped over that line."

Recollection of the incident still riles Junior. "I know what happened. Dale couldn't stand for Darrell to beat him with a pass that late in the race," says Junior. "So he pulled an old dirt-track trick on Darrell. Dale had been a good dirt track racer in his early days. He'd learned from his daddy. What Dale did is this: When Darrell went almost by him, Dale just kept his left front wheel at a point where Darrell's car wouldn't take a set to get through the corner. See, you've got to cock the rear end out to get the

car to turn. Dale held his ground to where Darrell couldn't cock out the rear end. So to me, as much as I'd raced on dirt, it was clearly deliberate. Hell, in the early years, I had used that technique myself. So don't tell me it was an accident."

Waltrip didn't win in 1986 until June 1, when he took a race at Riverside. It was the deepest into a season the team had gone without a victory since Darrell joined Junior. Only two more triumphs followed, at Bristol in August and at North Wilkesboro in September. His North Wilkesboro win cut Earnhardt's championship lead to 122 points. Waltrip cranked up his trademark rhetoric as he told the press, "I'd put some psychological stuff in the papers, but it wouldn't do any good because Dale and his boys can't read."

A few days later at Charlotte Motor Speedway, Earnhardt responded, "I can read. Just like in a kid's early reading book, 'See Darrell run his mouth. See Darrell fall.'"

And, of course, he did fall. Waltrip finished a distant second to Earnhardt in the championship chase, trailing by 288 points. Bonnett won for Junior in October at Rockingham and wound up thirteenth in the standings.

The late-season victories were going-away gifts from the Johnson teams. Neither driver would be with Junior in 1987. On June 27 of 1986, the *Charlotte Observer* broke the stunning news that Waltrip would leave Junior in 1987 for Hendrick Motorsports, where he'd be joined by veteran engine-builder/crew chief Waddell Wilson. Owner Rick Hendrick termed it a "dream team." A bit later Bonnett revealed that he would be rejoining the Rahmoc operation in 1987.

Waltrip, Hendrick, and Wilson, who was leaving the Ranier Racing team, made their troika official during a staged production at an Atlanta hotel in November. The

Junior and the team gave Waltrip a push late in the season, winning at Bristol in August and North Wilkesboro in September. But it wasn't enough for Waltrip to overtake Earnhardt for the championship, coming in second by 288 points. (David Chobat)

Junior and Waltrip remain close, here
posing in the Bristol garage in 1997.
"The time I was with Junior rates as the
best six years of my racing career," says
Waltrip. "Without Junior, I might have
been just another race-car driver."
(David Chobat)

# "Looking at the big picture with hindsight, I feel that if I'd stayed with Junior, we'd have won a lot more races."

show included Waltrip driving the racecar into view through a cloud of smoke. Waltrip had won three Winston Cup championships, forty-three races, and approximately $5.8 million in the cars owned and fielded by Junior Johnson. So it astonished most attending the press conference to hear Darrell say, after leaning down to kiss the hood of the Hendrick car, "I'm getting off an ol' mule and onto a good, strong thoroughbred."

Retorted Junior, "I've had a jackass driving my car, and now I'm rid of him."

Darrell Waltrip's jump to Hendrick Motorsports did not catch Junior by surprise. "I knew it was coming. I've got a lot of friends in the sport and in the businesses connected to the sport," says Junior. "I was tipped off to the whole deal early on. What Rick Hendrick wanted, as much as he wanted Darrell, was the Budweiser sponsorship. The Bud officials were good, solid people who kept their word. Rick thought Darrell could bring Bud's backing with him. I guess Darrell thought that, too. What they didn't know was that before Warner Hodgdon left racing, me and him went to St. Louis. We negotiated an extension of the sponsorship deal through at least 1989. Budweiser's contract was with me, not Darrell, and they weren't about to break it."

Waltrip was to spend four seasons with Hendrick before forming his own team in 1991. He won nine races for Hendrick Motorsports, his biggest victory coming in the 1989 Daytona 500. Waltrip's best showing in a points championship while driving for Hendrick was fourth place, achieved in 1987 and again in 1989.

"The time I was with Junior rate as the best six years of my racing career," Waltrip says in reflection. "Except for Junior, I might have been just another racecar driver. Thanks to the opportunity he gave me, and what we built

on together, I'm able to say, 'Boys, there ain't much in Winston Cup racing that I ain't done.' "

"Looking at the big picture with hindsight, I feel that if I'd stayed with Junior, we'd have won a lot more races, and we even might have more championships than anybody else.

"Among the things I admire most about Junior is that when he decided he wanted our team to really, really achieve something, he became totally committed. He was big into firsts. He deeply wanted to win the first Winston all-star race. And he wanted to be the first team owner to sit at the head table, the championship team's table, at the Waldorf-Astoria in New York. It's a measure of his dedication and leadership that we were able to do both of these things."

Junior had wrapped up six championships as a team owner, three with Yarborough and three with Waltrip, all in a glorious eight-year span. "Goodness, those were good years with those two," Junior says. "I really enjoyed both of those boys, and I count them as two of the best friends I've got. I'm getting a great kick out of teasing Cale and Darrell about that *Sports Illustrated* magazine article rating the twelve top drivers of all time. (Junior was rated first, Waltrip sixth, and Yarborough seventh.) I always told both of 'em that I could outdrive their asses. Now, I tell them, the *Sports Illustrated* thing proves it."

# CHAPTER SEVENTEEN

Junior's top choice to succeed Waltrip for the 1987 season was none other than Earnhardt. Never mind the anger ignited by the crash the year before.

"I'd hoped to hire Dale someday, and he'd always wanted to drive for me," says Junior. "I had done a lot of favors for Richard Childress through the years, both when he was driving and then when he concentrated on becoming a team owner. I got him and Dale together and got them a sponsor. So I didn't feel bad about offering Dale my ride. To my surprise, the Budweiser people did not want Earnhardt as a driver, although he'd just won a second championship and obviously was going to win a lot more. To this day I don't know why they were against me hiring Dale. They simply wanted me to get somebody else, so me and Terry Labonte got together. If I had it to do over, I'd have hired Dale anyway and found a second sponsor for his team while putting Labonte in the Bud car. I think me and Dale would have done real well together."

Labonte's success as a driver had been built with a team owned by Billy Hagan. Hagan spotted Labonte's talent, honed on the short tracks around Labonte's Corpus Christi, Texas, home, and brought him into Winston Cup racing for five races in 1978. Labonte won his first career

## "It's been well worth it."

Above right: Terry Labonte won only four races over three years with Junior, one of which was his victory at Pocono in the 1989 Miller 500. It was Junior's first win on a superspeedway since Neil Bonnett won at Rockingham in 1986. On the right is Ford's engineer for NASCAR, Preston Miller. (Dozier Mobley)

Opposite: Junior's crew erupts as Labonte wins the 1988 Winston at Charlotte Motor Speedway. Mike Hill, one of Junior's top mechanics, is in the foreground, just in front of crew member Randy Moose. (NASCAR Winston Cup Scene Archives)

**Bodine was a Yankee in a dominantly Southern sport. Now he was going to race for a man born and bred in the foothills of North Carolina's Brushy Mountains.**

race in the treacherous Southern 500 in 1980, cementing his standing as a winning driver and rising star.

Labonte established himself as one of NASCAR's premier drivers in 1984, when he claimed the Winston Cup Championship with two victories and a record of consistency: six runner-up finishes, six in third place, two in fourth, one in fifth, and seven from sixth through tenth.

He spent two more seasons with Hagan, until the team's poor financial situation forced him to look elsewhere for employment.

Labonte might not have found it with Junior had not Junior's sponsor, Budweiser, urged him to hire the Texan. "It's true," Junior says. "Not that we weren't interested in Terry, but of all the drivers we could tap at that particular time, it was a deal where Budweiser had been with Terry in prior years and had really liked him and his public relations association with them."

Labonte was a far cry from the outgoing, outlandish drivers Junior had previously employed. Labonte was nicknamed "The Iceman" for his calm, calculating demeanor on the track. But in reality, the name stuck because he was quiet, even reticent.

Junior liked Labonte's demeanor. For the three years Labonte drove for him, there were few, if any, outbreaks of emotion. Things were at least calm internally, even if they were unspectacular on the track.

"Terry was unique," Junior says. "He took every day of his racing in stride. It didn't make any difference what kind of trouble he had. He didn't blame anybody for what went on. He took the blame for what he did. He let other people do the same thing."

The three years Labonte spent with Junior produced just four victories—a far cry from the records of previous seasons. Yet Junior seemed content. That was because he

felt he had a good working relationship with Labonte. Better results, he reasoned, would come as their relationship grew. But they didn't. At the end of the 1989 season, Labonte left.

"Things were OK with Junior," Labonte says. "But it didn't seem like we were going anywhere. I wish we could have won more, I really do. I just didn't think we were going to get much better together so I thought it was best for me to move on."

Junior says, "We didn't win as much as I would have liked, but even with the blossom years earlier, I have to say I did better financially with Terry than any other driver I ever had. So it was a deal where you enjoy winning and all the glory that goes along with it, but you still enjoy the financial side of it."

In 1990, Junior hired Geoff Bodine to be his driver.

At the time, people scratched their heads because their personalities were diametrically opposed.

Bodine was mercurial—even, as some claimed, a bit strange. Perhaps that was because Bodine hailed from upstate New York and was a Yankee in a dominantly Southern sport. Now he was going to race for a man born and bred in the foothills of North Carolina's Brushy Mountains.

Still, Bodine could drive—and build—a racecar. A former standout on NASCAR's Modified circuit, Bodine had gotten his big Winston Cup break with Hendrick in 1984, and after six seasons with the Charlotte auto magnate's operation, had won seven races. But by 1989, Bodine had been replaced as the star of Hendrick's three-car operation by Waltrip, who won six times that year to just once for Bodine. When the opportunity to join Junior arose, Bodine took it.

Junior knew Bodine's personality, but despite what reservations he might have had, he admired him as a driver

Junior surprised many observers when he hired New England driver Geoff Bodine in 1990. "When he first came to us, I tell you, he was hard to handle by anybody's standards," says Junior. (David Chobat)

In 1991 Junior expanded to a two-car operation for the second time in his career, hiring Sterling Marlin. The son of former NASCAR racer Coo Coo Marlin, Sterling lasted two years with Junior, but never won a race. (David Chobat)

and felt that was enough to warrant hiring him. There was a period of adjustment, of course. Bodine had his ideas on how things should be done, but they didn't always mesh with the policies and practices long upheld by the managers and crew at Junior Johnson and Associates.

"When he first came to us, I tell you, he was hard to handle by anybody's standards," Junior says. "The relationship between him and my crew chief, Tim Brewer, who wasn't afraid to stand by his opinions, either, eventually broke down, and it never really seemed to work from that point on."

Despite the skepticism many felt about a Junior-Bodine union, the 1990 season produced three victories, the most for Junior's team since Waltrip won three in 1986. That, perhaps as much as anything else, prompted Junior to extend Bodine's employment into 1991. But there was a major difference. For the second time in his career as an owner, Junior ran a second team.

"I was having a problem with a few things," Junior says. "A one-team operation was difficult to finance, given everything you had to do in racing to keep up. You had to test extensively, you had to do research and development work. You couldn't do that with just one team. There were just so many things you had to do that one team could not afford to do."

Junior's thinking was that if he had a second team, expenses could be contained by sharing testing information. One team could perform research and development and report the results to the other, giving both the benefits at the cost of one.

A multicar team was the kind of operation Bodine had left after the end of the 1989 season. He didn't welcome a new one.

"No driver wants to be in a two-car team," Junior says. "I don't know if they express that as much now as they used to, but back then, it was a no-no from the go-go."

Maxwell House Coffee entered NASCAR as the sponsor of Junior's second team, with Sterling Marlin as the driver. Marlin enjoyed productive seasons with Junior, despite the fact he did not win. But he was not the first choice. If Junior had been able to hire the driver he wanted, it would have been Alan Kulwicki, a college-educated competitor whose tenacious determination propelled him into the winner's circle four short years after he had come into Winston Cup racing from Wisconsin. He was the rarest of the rare. He not only drove, he owned his own team.

Junior, like everyone else, had watched Kulwicki doggedly overcome one obstacle after another to pursue his dream to race on his terms. Junior admired him and his skills as a driver, mechanic, and businessman. With the creation of a second team, Junior felt he was in a position to offer Kulwicki a unique opportunity that would benefit them both.

"I knew how underfinanced he was," Junior says. "And seeing him do with his team what he did under those circumstances, I knew he was a hard-working, determined type of man. Now, you take that and put it with a good race team and give him a little time off from everything he had to do, well, you've got a superstar."

At the time, Kulwicki was negotiating to acquire a sponsor for his team, which would be in trouble if he could not land one in time for the 1991 season. That was another reason Junior felt he could entice the future Winston Cup champion to drive for him.

Junior made handsome offers to Kulwicki. "I was determined to get him," Junior says. "But it got down to the point where I was looking at my sponsor and the money I had to pay a driver. It got to the point where there was a limit to what I could pay." So Junior gave up and turned to Marlin.

Kulwicki concluded that he could best serve himself by remaining independent. People thought he was crazy to burden himself with team ownership and all the pressure it brings when he could drive for one of the foremost team owners and make a lot of money.

Kulwicki's resistance to Junior's offers intensified when he was convinced he had landed a sponsor. In fact, he hadn't. Maxwell House was the sponsor Kulwicki thought he had on the hook, and it had already signed with Junior.

Two things influenced Kulwicki's decision to turn him down, says Junior. First, Kulwicki was getting advice from fellow team owner Felix Sabates, the flamboyant, wealthy Cuban who served as his mentor. Second, Kulwicki was convinced he could continue his own operation because a sponsor was coming on board. When Kulwicki refused him, Junior understood.

Alan Kulwicki gained serious attention from team owners after winning races like the 1990 AC-Delco 500 in Rockingham. Junior was so impressed by the self-financed driver that he tried repeatedly to convince Kulwicki to drive for him in 1991. (David Chobat)

**"What happened in that whole deal was purely a freak thing," Junior says. "It was just a mistake; that's basically it, because if I was going to cheat, it would have been pretty deep."**

"I don't know what the Maxwell House people had told him," Junior says, "but I already had a contract with them. I told him he just wasn't going to get that sponsor. I don't know if he ever believed me."

Junior says he would still be in racing today if Kulwicki had driven for him, that Kulwicki's determination and mechanical skills would have blended nicely with his own.

"You wouldn't have needed that guy they call the chief mechanic that everyone hangs their hat on," Junior says. "All you would need was a craftsman at putting a car together, making sure it didn't fall apart, and Alan would have done the rest of it."

Kulwicki, in time, acquired another sponsor and continued to run his own team. He earned the admiration of race fans everywhere when he won the Winston Cup championship in 1992. He died, tragically, in a plane crash in Blountville, Tennessee, on April 1, 1993.

With Bodine and Marlin aboard, Junior's teams began competition in 1991 with high hopes that much could be gained from the expanded operation. But if Junior gained anything by having two teams, the records didn't show it.

It was a season tainted by controversy, with Junior's team the target.

The Winston, the special all-star race run on May 19 at Charlotte Motor Speedway, was the scene of a major disruption when NASCAR discovered an oversized engine in Junior's Ford.

The car was driven by Tommy Ellis, a gritty Virginian who had won a NASCAR Busch Series championship and was the substitute for Bodine, who had suffered a punctured lung and three cracked ribs in a crash during practice.

Three hours after the race was over, NASCAR announced that Junior's Ford, which had finished fourteenth among the twenty entries, was equipped with an oversized engine. The engine measured 362.351 cubic inches, well above the 358-cubic-inch maximum.

Junior and crew chief Brewer were suspended for four races.

"What happened in that whole deal was purely a freak thing," Junior says. "J.V. Reins [another of Junior's engine builders] was building two engines at the same time. Because of the limitations on good engine blocks at that time, we couldn't afford to give up a block if it was a little bit oversized."

One of the engines Reins prepared had a longer stroke and smaller bore, while the other had a shorter stroke and a bigger bore. According to Junior, Reins mistakenly put the long-stroke crankshaft in the large-bore block. The other motor had the wrong crankshaft, too, except its displacement was undersized rather than oversized.

"We rattled around as close to the size as we could get," Junior says, "because you couldn't afford to leave anything on the table. It was just a mistake; that's basically it. If it had been intentional, there probably wouldn't have been enough paper to put the size down on, because if I was going to cheat, it would have been pretty deep."

NASCAR's severe ruling bothered Junior because it was enforced despite the fact that the Winston was a special race, an event not listed as an official Winston Cup event, and one that did not award points.

Junior says, "Not only that, but we didn't take away from anyone else. We finished so far back in the race [won by Davey Allison] that it just didn't matter. I felt the penalty was a grudge penalty. It wasn't nothing else."

Junior got around the suspensions by listing his wife Flossie as the team owner and changing the car's familiar No. 11 to No. 97. That continued until June 23 at Michigan Speedway, where the No. 11 car returned to

Bodine leads Ken Shrader (25) and Hut Strickland (12) into turn one at Charlotte Motor Speedway during the 1991 Mello Yello 500. Bodine completed the final 114 laps without pitting, and led the last sixteen. No other team could run for as many laps without refueling, which prompted speculation that Bodine's tank was illegal. (Don Hunter)

the track. Bodine's recuperation lasted two races, and he was back in action at Sonoma, California, three weeks after the Winston.

Bodine earned just one Winston Cup victory, in the Mello Yello 500, in October at Charlotte. Remarkably, even that was tainted. Competing teams suspected Bodine's Ford carried an illegal gas tank, one that held more than the allowed twenty-two gallons.

Suspicion was aroused after Bodine completed the last 114 of 500 miles without refueling, a distance other drivers could not match. His strongest challenger, front-runner Davey Allison, who drove a Ford for owner Robert Yates, was forced to pit for fuel with seventeen laps remaining. That allowed Bodine to take the lead he would hold for the remainder of the race. Bodine eased off the throttle for the final ten laps to conserve what fuel he had.

If there was something altered in Bodine's fuel tank, it was never revealed. After conducting a post-race inspection, NASCAR was satisfied that the tank was not illegal.

It let the matter drop despite the speculation of a few that Bodine's Ford could carry more than a gallon over the legal limit.

Crew chief Brewer explained that better mileage was attained by using a conservative rear-end gear.

The season ended three races later.

Dale Earnhardt claimed his fifth championship, while Bodine finished fourteenth in the final point standings and Marlin seventh, despite the fact he hadn't won a race.

"I really can't say a bad thing about those days with J.J.," Bodine says. "Those were good years. Yeah, I wish we could have done more. But still, it was a good time in my career."

**Right:** Junior and Lisa with daughter Meredith Suzanne, and son Robert Glenn III, sit on the steps of their current home in Yadkin County. "We have our life together, and it is what we want and enjoy," says Lisa. (NASCAR Winston Cup Scene Archives)

**Opposite:** The Charlotte win was Bodine's only victory of the season. Competitors wondered how Bodine's car could run so many laps on one tank of gas, so NASCAR ordered an inspection. News reporters were ushered away and Junior's crew obstructed the view of the gas pump. Davey Allison's crew chief, Larry McReynolds, contended he saw the meter read 23.2 gallons, 1.2 more than legal capacity. Nevertheless, NASCAR ruled that the car was legal. (David Chobat)

Although from 1987 through 1991, Junior always had a driver among the top ten in the final point standings—something most team owners coveted—it was a far cry from what had been accomplished in earlier years.

In 1991, Junior and Flossie began divorce proceedings. It was Junior's decision. Stories about what prompted his decision have been, and continue to be, the subject of gossip within NASCAR. Junior expected that, especially because he became associated with a woman younger by more than thirty years.

"I knew what the consequences would be," Junior says. "I knew there would be a lot of repercussions. But I was willing to accept that."

The divorce was costly. Flossie acquired their home and one of the adjoining shops, among other things. And of his three sisters, the only other family he has left, two haven't spoken to him since, though he remains on good terms with his sister Annie Mae. But after a year's separation, required by North Carolina law, the divorce was official on October 27, 1992.

"I didn't want to hurt anybody," Junior says. "In fact, I wanted Flossie to have half of everything we had. And I was willing to give that to her. But she had some lawyers who thought she could get it all. We had a lot of trouble in that respect, but we worked it all out."

Junior married the former Lisa Day, a vivacious strawberry blonde, on November 17, 1992. Junior had known her all her life. She grew up a half-mile from his home and became a registered nurse in the cardiology department at Baptist Hospital in Winston-Salem.

While they knew each other for almost all of Lisa's life, for years they were nothing more than friends. Then their relationship developed into something more. They were friends who fell in love.

Contrary to some speculation, Junior's decision to divorce was based on his feelings for Lisa, not because he was desperate for children.

"It never bothered me that I didn't have children," Junior says. "I always had a lot of kids around. I took a lot of interest in my brothers' and sisters' kids.

"Lisa and I started dating after I left home. And then I knew what I wanted. I knew what it was going to take to reverse my life. I knew what kind of criticisms I would hear, but I didn't care. And it's been well worth it."

They knew what people would say given the difference in their ages, but it didn't matter.

"There is one thing Lisa and I agreed upon a long time ago," Junior says. "We weren't going to get into a war of criticism or talking about people and making accusations about who they were, what they did, and what they should have done with their lives. We wanted no part of that.

"I have never said anything bad about Flossie, and I ain't going to. And not about anyone else, as far as that goes. We won't stoop to that level.

"We have had nasty, dirty stuff said about us, and I expected that. I've had stuff said about me all my life. Someone's jealous, or something like that, and they say something to someone, who says something else to someone else, and before you know it, it's all blowed up to the point where nothing is true."

"Junior and I are very happy," Lisa says. "We don't have a hidden agenda;, we never did. We have our life together, and it is what we want and enjoy."

Junior says, "I'm not ashamed of my life. I'm sure it's not the best life that's ever been lived. If I've ever hurt anyone, it's because I wanted to live my life the way I wanted and not the way others wanted me to. I won't do that."

# CHAPTER EIGHTEEN

In 1992, another championship was within Junior's grasp.

At the end of the 1991 season, Bodine had departed; Marlin remained. Bodine's replacement on the two-car team was Bill Elliott, the type of driver everyone thought would help Junior return to the on-track success he enjoyed with Allison, Yarborough, and Waltrip.

Elliott came with impeccable credentials. He was the 1988 Winston Cup champion. He had won eleven superspeedway races in 1985, the same year he won the Winston Million, a $1 million bonus for winning three of four selected races. And he was wildly popular.

Elliott's rise to success was fueled by his association with Harry Melling, a Michigan businessman who put Elliott behind the wheel of his Ford in 1982. A year later, Elliott, a lanky, red-haired Georgian, won his first career race. He won three more in 1984 and eleven in 1985, and never failed to win at least one race with Melling through

## "Bill is the right kind of driver to win championships."

Above right: **Bill Elliott left his Melling team and joined Junior in 1992, driving the No. 11 Budweiser car. Four years earlier, "Awesome Bill from Dawsonville" had won the championship and the Winston Million. (David Chobat)**

Opposite: **Miscommunication between the pit and Elliott may have cost the team the 1992 championship in Atlanta. "He was on the radio, and he kept asking, 'When are we going to pit? When are we going to pit?' When Tim would talk back to him, Bill didn't seem to understand," Junior explains. (David Chobat)**

Left: Elliott won his fourth straight race of the season after taking the TranSouth 500 at Darlington. He led the last 45 laps and held off a hard-charging Harry Gant down the stretch. Because of NASCAR's point system, Elliott was second to Davey Allison in the overall standings even though he had won four of the season's first five races. (David Chobat)

Opposite: Elliott went on to win an anti-climactic Hooters 500 in Atlanta. Kulwicki placed second and led the most laps (the result of Elliott's early pit stop), which allowed him to take the championship by the closest margin in NASCAR history, 10 points. (David Chobat)

1991. In fact, he had won six races in both the 1987 and 1988 seasons.

By the end of 1991, Elliott split with his brothers, Ernie and Dan, who worked on the Melling team.

"It was a good time to move on," Elliott says. "We had done a lot with Melling, but it just seemed my brothers and I were sorta taking different directions. We felt it was best if we did different things.

"My career was made with Harry Melling, there's no doubt about that. But when the time came to make a move, I figured I couldn't do any better than to join Junior."

"I talked to Bill quite a bit back in the mid-'80s," Junior says. "A time or two, I thought I was awful close to signing him as my driver. He had been with Melling for so long and they had been so successful that Bill felt he owed Melling a lot and he wanted to repay that, even if he might have felt he wanted to go somewhere else. I couldn't blame him for that."

At the beginning of the 1992 campaign, Junior thought he had the driver it took to win a title.

"Bill is the right kind of driver to win championships," he said at the time.

The new team got off to a great start. Elliott won four of the first five races of the season—at Rockingham, Richmond, Atlanta, and Darlington. Despite that, he wasn't atop the point standings. The NASCAR point system, considered by many to be one of the quirkiest in professional sports, rewards consistency and pays bonus points for leading laps. That makes it possible for a driver to win more races than any other and still not lead the point standings or win the championship.

At the end of his four-for-five streak, Elliott was forty-eight points behind Davey Allison. How he got to the top of the point standings again illustrates the foibles of the NASCAR point system. At Pocono, Pennsylvania, Elliott finished thirteenth but took the points lead after going winless in eleven straight races. Allison placed thirty-third.

Going into the Pyroil 500 at Phoenix International Raceway, the next-to-last race of the season, Elliott had a seventy-point lead over Allison and was eighty-five points ahead of Kulwicki. The margin was slim, so that any measure of bad luck for any of the contenders would take them out of the running.

Elliott started the race eighteenth, and after only a few laps, his Ford began smoking. The engine had blown a head gasket. Several pit stops failed to correct the problem, and Elliott was forced to limp around the one-mile track to a thirty-first-place finish.

Allison, meanwhile, sped to victory, while Kulwicki wound up fourth.

The team later discovered that the piece of machinery that milled the cylinder heads didn't mill the heads smoothly. It essentially gouged the head, which caused the head gasket to fail.

"Basically, what happened at Phoenix wasn't anybody's fault," Junior says.

The Phoenix disaster meant that Allison had a thirty-point lead over Kulwicki and forty over Elliott, who had dropped from first place to third. Still, the championship was within grasp. It came down to the season finale, the Hooters 500 at Atlanta Motor Speedway on November 15.

If the championship battle wasn't enough to create great anticipation for the Hooters 500, the race was also the final stop for Richard Petty's Fan Appreciation Tour. The seven-time Winston Cup champion and acknowledged king of the sport was going to race for the last time.

Petty was a focal point for the fans' attention. But the championship contenders were under more intense scrutiny. To win the title, all Allison had to do was finish sixth or better. The only tactic available to Elliott and Kulwicki was to run their Fords to the limit and hope that Allison faltered.

While running comfortably in fifth place, Allison was caught up in an accident caused when Ernie Irvan spun coming out of the fourth turn on lap 254 of 328. Extensive repairs were done to Allison's Ford, but he was out of championship contention with a twenty-seventh-place finish.

Meanwhile, Elliott was doing exactly what was required of him. He sped into the lead by lap sixty-two, swapped it with Kulwicki and then ran off a long string of laps led.

When Elliott pitted on lap 210, Kulwicki inherited the lead. As part of his strategy, Kulwicki planned to keep that lead as long as he could. He had calculated how many laps he would have to lead in order to lead the most laps in the race and gain the five-point bonus from NASCAR's point system. He led laps 210 through 310, with Elliott right behind him.

When Kulwicki pitted on lap 311, Elliott moved into first place and then pitted on lap 314.

It was too early.

"Our radios, for some reason, weren't connecting good with Bill on the track," Junior says. "He was on the radio, and he kept asking, 'When are we going to pit? When are we going to pit?' When Tim would talk back to him, Bill didn't seem to understand. He'd come back and say, 'Did you say pit? When do you want me to pit?' It was kinda confusing."

Had Elliott pitted two laps later, the championship outcome would have been different. When Junior saw Elliott come down pit road two laps early, he knew he had lost the championship unless something happened to Kulwicki.

Out of the pits, Elliott moved back into the lead on lap 316 and led the rest of the way, with Kulwicki in second place. It was Elliott's fifth victory of the year. But it was a hollow one. Kulwicki's second-place finish, coupled with the bonus points for leading the most laps, gave him the Winston Cup championship by ten points (4,078 to 4,068), the closest margin in NASCAR history.

Kulwicki led 103 laps, the number he knew he had to acquire in order to lead the most laps in the race. Elliott led 102. Elliott and Kulwicki each earned 180 points in the race. Had Elliott led the most laps, he would have received 185 points to 175 for Kulwicki and they would have tied for the championship. The tie-breaker is the number of victories for each driver. Elliott had five, Kulwicki two. Elliott would have been the champion.

As he looked back on the race, Junior realized he should have taken a firmer hand in the pits. But rather than blame any individual, he chose to call the defeat a "team loss," though not long after the race he dismissed crew chief Tim Brewer.

"I blame myself because I could have gotten on the radio and directed Bill," Junior said. "But before I could do that, here he comes down pit road. When I saw that, it reached the point where I just didn't care what happened. I knew we had lost the championship."

After Victory Lane ceremonies, which were dampened by the loss of the championship, Junior went on back to the motel and got out of Atlanta as quickly as he could.

The end of the 1992 season was a major disappointment but had been the best competitive year for Junior's teams since Waltrip won seven races in 1984. It showed the

**Right:** All of Junior's crewmen leapt into the pool at their motel in Daytona Beach after Spencer won the Pepsi 400. (NASCAR Winston Cup Scene Archives)

**Opposite:** In 1994 Jimmy Spencer replaced Strickland and brought Junior back to Victory Lane twice, with the biggest win coming at the Pepsi 400 in Daytona. Holding young Robert Glenn III, Lisa shared in the Victory Lane celebration. (David Chobat)

quality of the Junior-Elliott association and that perhaps a championship could still be won.

In 1993, Junior acquired McDonald's sponsorship and teamed the company with a new driver, Hut Stricklin, an Alabama native who had spent the better part of the previous two seasons driving for Bobby Allison's team.

Early in the year, Junior underwent heart surgery. It had surprised just about everyone in racing, including the press, since no one had heard of any problems. He simply slipped away, had the procedure done, and returned.

The surgery took place three days after the GM Goodwrench 500 at North Carolina Motor Speedway in Rockingham, North Carolina, on February 28. Junior had dealt with bouts of what he described as indigestion, a burning sensation in his chest soon after eating. He and Lisa were alarmed because Junior had been diagnosed with artery blockage on two separate occasions since 1975. Doctors at Duke University Hospital said he did have blockage and that they were going to do an angioplasty.

"One of his main arteries [the one under his left arm] was crooked so badly it was almost L-shaped; they couldn't get the needle through it," Lisa says. "They had tried to do the angioplasty for four or five hours and couldn't get it done, so they came back out, at night, and talked about doing a bypass."

The next morning, Junior underwent the procedure. He recovered from surgery so well that he was home in four days instead of the expected seven. He went back to the shop two days after returning home. He was back at the track at Darlington on March 28, just twenty-five days after reporting to the hospital.

The season, unlike Junior's health, did not improve.

There was pressure from sponsors to improve the team's performance. They brought up the terrific Elliott streak of four wins in the first five races of 1992.

"What happened in 1992 didn't have anything to do with what happened in 1993," Junior says. "Budweiser wanted me to cave in and reacquire Tim. But that wasn't going to happen."

Junior's relationship with his longtime sponsor slowly began to crumble.

"It wasn't a working relationship for most of the season," Junior says. "About two-thirds through the season, the Budweiser guys were telling Bill to go back home and form his own team and they would sponsor him."

That didn't happen, however, and Budweiser remained with Junior.

The year turned out to be the dimmest of Junior's career as a team owner. A championship wasn't even approached. In fact, neither Elliott nor Stricklin won a race. It marked the first time since 1966 that a Junior-owned team failed to win at least once; a span of twenty-seven years.

Victories returned in 1994.

Elliott's new teammate was Jimmy Spencer, a former Modified driver whose aggressiveness and "Mr. Excitement" nickname had become well-known among competitors.

Elliott won once, in the prestigious Southern 500 at Darlington and Spencer won twice, in the Pepsi 400 at Daytona and the DieHard 500 at Talladega, both in July. But by the close of the season, Junior knew his sponsors were leaving and that his days of multicar ownership were at an end.

"Our contracts were up for negotiations at the end of 1994, and McDonald's came back to me with an incentive deal for 1995," Junior says. The incentive program meant that sponsorship was contingent upon performance. Junior's team had to win a certain number of poles and a certain number of races to receive money.

Spencer (27) and Elliott (11) lead Mark
Martin (6) during the 1994 First Union
400 at North Wilkesboro. Spencer
placed twenty-third and Elliott finished
sixth. Martin finished fifth in his
Valvoline Ford. (David Chobat)

"I couldn't take a deal like that," Junior says. "There are very few people who could take a deal like that. I don't know anyone who is a businessperson who could. I had been given a choice of take it or leave it, and I left it. Budweiser had already made a deal with Bill for the '95 season, but when McDonald's came free, he dropped Budweiser for the McDonald's deal, and that's how it came to an end with me."

At the end of 1994, Junior had to acquire a sponsor and hire a driver if he wanted to keep on racing. Although there were a few other possibilities, Junior and Lowe's, a hardware firm that was founded in North Wilkesboro, reached an agreement. Spencer could have stayed on as Junior's driver, but Lowe's preferred Brett Bodine, Geoff's younger brother, because of his public relations skills.

Junior entered the 1995 season without much enthusiasm. He rated his team's potential as "low." He seemed to sense that an end was near. Bodine and Mike Beam, the team's crew chief, were often at odds. About halfway through the season, Beam departed to become Elliott's crew chief. Dean Combs replaced him.

Junior says: "Dean did a good job for us, but by the time he came on, it was too far gone for anyone to save."

The season was mediocre. Bodine finished among the top ten only twice in thirty-one races. Junior began to ponder retirement. The idea was not new to him. He would have gotten out after 1985 if Warner Hodgdon had purchased his team. On the other hand, if he had retained McDonald's as his sponsor, he might have pressed on beyond 1995.

"I had everything it took to race, but when Budweiser left and then McDonald's offered me that incentive deal, that disturbed me," Junior says. "I was ready to get out then. And some of my people had gotten to the point

**"Junior got tired of haggling. He could do one of two things. He could take the sponsors' lowball deal and suffer competitively, or he could get out of racing.**

where they didn't care any more, although I did have some good people. Lowe's was a good sponsor. But we couldn't win for them. I saw that right away."

Junior got his opportunity to get out when Bodine came to him about halfway through the 1995 season and asked if Junior would be willing to sell the team.

"I said, 'Sure, I'll sell the team.' I've sold it twice before and got it back," Junior says. "So I'll sell it again."

"What I tried to do was to base my race team on all the money I was paid for sponsorship. I plowed all my resource money into the team and hoped I could win enough to be OK. But when I had to start taking all my winnings and plow them back in and then go into my pocket because I didn't have sufficient sponsorship to keep it afloat, why, there were only two things I could do. I could sell the team or shut it down. I chose to sell it, because it's not profitable to shut a team down."

Junior had already made one sale, at the end of 1994. He had sold what had been the McDonald's-backed team to Bob Brooks, CEO of the Hooters restaurant chain.

Bodine, Lowe's, and Junior entered into negotiations.

"Lowe's felt Brett could turn it around if he owned the team and had the say-so to do what he wanted," Junior says. "So the deal was to put Lowe's money behind Brett and let him run with it. Basically, I was selling the team to Lowe's. They were the ones asking me how much it would cost to buy the team. That was fine with me."

The sale was made official on November 22, 1995, when Junior and Bodine signed a contract. Bodine, with his Lowe's sponsorship money, bought everything—trucks, cars, equipment, motors, anything that was inside the shops.

"I felt it was the right thing for me to do," Bodine says. "Things had gone badly. Mike was a good guy, but we weren't getting along, and when he left, I could see things were getting no better.

"I knew Junior wanted to sell. Guys in suits had been coming to the shops. I discussed buying the team with my wife, Diane, and we came to Junior with an offer. I think he really wanted me to have it more than someone from the outside. Junior was ready to get out."

After the sale to Bodine, Junior didn't feel any temptation to return to racing.

"Racing had become a business, and when I was real successful racing, I wasn't in the business side as much as I was in the knowledgeable side. I knew what it took to make cars go fast," Junior says.

When racing took Junior out of his element, he became less effective as a team owner. He knew what it cost to run a team, but sponsors came with lower offers. Junior got tired of haggling. He could do one of two things. He could take the sponsors' lowball deal and suffer competitively, or he could get out of racing.

"I chose to get out," Junior says.

Except for a later sale in which he acquired some equipment for his farm, Junior never went back to his shops after they were gutted in the sale to Bodine.

"Never looked back," he says.

Once Junior left racing, he was gone for good. After selling his team to Bodine he stopped attending Winston Cup events and did not visit his former race shop. "Never looked back," he says. (NASCAR Winston Cup Scene Archives)

Though his time is mostly spent with his family, Junior also manages the crops and cattle on his 300-acre farm. (Don Hunter)

During the mid and late seventies, this style Junior Johnson and Associates patch was used on team uniforms. It was an era dominated by Junior and his team. They won three consecutive Winston Cup championships in 1976, 1977, and 1978. And in 1977, Cale Yarborough finished all thirty races, which was an unprecedented achievement in the modern era.

# EPILOGUE

The columned, stately home of Junior, Lisa, and their children sits atop a hill facing "old U.S. 421," a main highway of Yadkin County. It's the road Junior started on for virtually all the liquor-hauling runs that were to make him one of the most colorful characters in the moonshining folklore of the Carolinas and the rest of Dixie.

Junior's land is dotted with trees and sprawls across rolling hills. It's home to 700 head of Black Angus cattle. His estate is a far cry from the rugged back roads he traversed as a moonshiner or the ovals of dirt and asphalt on which he forged his considerable reputation as a stock car driver.

Today, Junior's time is divided between working his 300-acre farm and raising his family, Robert Glenn III, age five, and Meredith Susanne, age three. "One of the reasons I left racing was to spend time with my children," Junior says. "I wanted to watch them grow up."

A devoted father, Junior was able to watch his son being born.

"Lisa was having a cesarean section, and she was a bit scared, as you might expect," says Junior. "When Robert was being taken from her, I was sitting there holding her hand. The doctor said, 'Would you like to see your son?' so I stood up and looked over the curtain and all I could see was his little head stickin' out of Lisa's belly. It was one of the great adventures of my life."

Most of Junior's immediate family is gone now. The redoubtable Robert Glenn Johnson died in 1965. One year later, Junior's mother, Lora Belle, passed away. L.P., his oldest brother, died in 1988. Brother Fred died in 1992. Annie Mae Johnson and Ruth Johnson Tucker reside in Winston-Salem. Shirley Johnson Blackman lives in Cary.

The year 1998 was one of important recognition for Junior. In addition to being named the greatest driver in NASCAR history by *Sports Illustrated*, he was named one of the fifty greatest drivers as part of the celebration of NASCAR's fiftieth anniversary. Also honored were Bobby Allison, Geoff Bodine, Bill Elliott, Darrell Waltrip, and Cale Yarborough, all of whom drove for Junior.

"It's a tough thing to talk about yourself and how you might want to be remembered," Junior says. "I think the biggest thing is that I tried to treat people fairly and was honest in what I felt I had to do.

"As a driver, you ruffle a lot of feathers, but you don't set out to hurt anyone. I raced a lot of great professionals, and I respected them. I would like to be remembered as one of the competitors who treated others fair and raced them fair. I tried to honor the sport of racing in every way I could. I never downgraded it.

"I certainly feel," Junior says slowly, "that I gave racing a lot more than I took from it."

In April 1965 Junior celebrates a dominant performance at his home track in North Wilkesboro. He led 356 of 400 laps. (Southern MotoRacing)